UNSTOPPABLE

A 5 STEP GUIDE TO RECLAIMING YOUR IDENTITY & PURPOSE

JACKIE HICKS

Unstoppable: A 5 step Guide to Reclaiming Identity & Purpose

Copyright © 2025 Jackie Hicks

All rights reserved. No part of this publication may be reproduced, distributed, or transmitted in any form or by any means, including photocopying, recording, or other electronic or mechanical methods, without the prior written permission of the publisher, except as permitted by U.S. copyright law. For permission requests, contact [include publisher/author contact info].

The story, all names, characters, and incidents portrayed in this production are fictitious. No identification with actual persons (living or deceased), places, buildings, and products is intended or should be inferred.

ISBN: 979-8-9928879-0-7

DEDICATION

This book is dedicated to my husband. Thank you for believing in me, reigniting my passion, and reminding me of God's goodness. I love you, and I couldn't have done this without you. To my Dad, I thank you for being my cheerleader, for always believing in me, and for showing and reminding me that I could do anything. I love you. For every struggle, for every pain, I am grateful. It has helped to shape who I am today. I wish my mom were here to see this in person, but I know she still believes in her little girl. Love you mama! I love you to my siblings and all of those who have shown me love and kindness through my most challenging moments. And finally, to all of you who will read this book. I dedicate it to you, to your future, and to you becoming Unstoppable.

Table of Contents

Introduction 1

What Do You Stand For? 5

Who Are You?: 10

The Fight: 23

But Am I Though? 32

What Do You Think: 43

Let It Go 51

Don't Hold Your Breath 61

Vision: It's a Whole New World: 69

Beast Mode: Hitting Back: 76

Pressure: Finishing Phase: 83

About The Author 89

Therapy Resources 89

References 90

Introduction

Have you ever looked at yourself in the mirror and thought, Who the hell am I? Not just in a passing... "I need to make some changes" kind of way, but in a deep, gut-wrenching, I don't even recognize myself anymore kind of way? That moment when you realize you've been walking through life on autopilot: detached, drained, and just existing but not really living?

Yeah. That was me. As a young girl and in my teenage years, I was footloose and fancy free. I had what I would like to think of as a healthy dose of skepticism, a healthy dose of belief. Day by day, life continued to happen. Betrayed by friends... check. Trust factor number one is gone, betrayed by another friend, and another, and another. Trust in women? Borderline nil. Boyfriend's best friend kidnaps and rapes me... (confusion). Good friend's boyfriend raped me in my bed while asleep... To hell with this, I'm out! No trust in anyone! And that wasn't even the end of it; It had only just begun...

Life didn't just knock me down. It levelled me. One moment, I thought I had everything under control, and the next, I was standing in the wreckage of who I used to be. Wondering where the hell it all went wrong. And that's the thing about trauma, it doesn't just hurt, it rewires you. It buries pieces of you under survival mode, making

Unstoppable: A 5 step Guide to Reclaiming Identity & Purpose

you begin to believe that the emptiness you feel is normal.

So, what did I do? I did what most people do. I kept moving. I kept grinding. I threw myself into work, into relationships, into whatever would keep me too distracted to deal with the black hole I felt inside. I told myself I was fine. I was functioning, right??? I was checking the boxes, showing up, and pretending like I had it all together. But deep down? I was faking every second of it.

And then, one day, someone asked me a question that changed everything: "But WHY???????

Why did I keep giving to people who only drained me?

Why did I keep saying yes when my soul was screaming 'no'?

Why was I so damned convinced that I wasn't enough despite everything I had overcome?

Why did I continue to need external validation?

Let me tell you, when you start asking yourself "But WHY?" You better get ready and brace for the truth because the truth will often wreck you before it rebuilds you.

After asking the question, I realized that I had been lying to myself for a long time. Here I am telling everyone that my biggest pet peeve, that the thing I hate the most, is a liar, and I had been lying to myself for years! I had built my entire identity around keeping other people happy, making sure everyone else had what they needed, while I ran on fumes. I had convinced myself that if I just worked harder, loved harder, and gave more, then maybe- just maybe, I'd finally feel whole. Spoiler alert: it doesn't work like that.

That question: WHY, haunted me no matter how much I tried to answer it. I finally began to realize that I no longer knew who I was. I spent so much time avoiding the wreckage, keeping busy, pouring into others, numbing myself with distractions, that I never stopped to acknowledge my own damage. I lost pieces of myself along the way, and I kept thinking that if I just worked harder, gave more, and stayed strong, it would all make sense again. But it never did. Remember, you can't run from yourself.

And the wake-up call was no-one was coming to save me either. There was no magical moment that would suddenly make me feel like myself again. If I wanted to reclaim my life, I had to do the work. That's where you are right now, isn't it? You feel it? The dissonance, the exhaustion, the quiet voice in your head telling you that something is off. So let me ask you... But why?

At some point, I had to turn around and face myself, and so will you. When you do, you realize there's no going back. We can't return to who we were before the trauma, before the heartbreak, before life knocked us down. That version of you is gone! But that doesn't mean you're lost forever; it means you get to rebuild.

And that's precisely what this book is about.

This is not a sugar-coated, feel-good message that suggests just thinking positive thoughts will make you fine. No, this is about real work. The raw, messy, uncomfortable, but absolutely necessary process of reclaiming yourself after life has torn you apart. It's about breaking free from the beliefs that have kept you small, rewriting the story you've been telling yourself, and stepping into the version of you that refuses to be held back.

I am not here to give you a magic formula because there isn't one. Healing isn't a straight line; it isn't linear. Some days you'll feel unstoppable, and other days, it will take everything in you to get out of bed. That's a part of the process. But if you're willing to fight for yourself, I promise you it is worth it.

Perhaps you picked up this book because you're tired of feeling stuck, or maybe you don't even know who you are anymore and are desperate to find out. Or maybe, just maybe, there is a part of you that knows you were meant for more, even if you don't quite believe it yet.

Whatever brings you here, know this: YOU ARE NOT ALONE!

I hope you see yourself in my story and the stories presented on these pages. As you read through these pages, I hope you find the courage to ask yourself the hard questions, to confront the feelings that have been holding you back, and to take the first steps toward the life you deserve.

Because no matter how lost you feel right now, I promise you, you are not broken! The life you want, the person you want to be. She's still in there. Waiting... and she is ready to fight back...Are you???

It's time to stop lying to yourself. It's time to RIP off the mask, to shatter the old narratives, and build something real. Because you deserve more than just survival. You deserve to live. So, I'll ask you one last time: but WHY? And this time, don't stop asking until you find the answer that sets you free.

Chapter One

What do You Stand For?

When I moved out on my own at the age of nineteen, I thought independence was just about paying bills and decorating my first place the way I wanted. But I quickly learned that living on your own comes with a much deeper responsibility: deciding who you're going to be when no one is watching. It was the first time my beliefs were tested, that my values weren't just ideals I agreed with, they were the compass that guided every choice I made. There was no parent in the next room to correct me, no one to set a curfew, no "don't do that" voice except my own. And yet there was still this pull inside me, a desire to maintain the "good girl" image I had grown up with.

When I was living in Macon, GA., I had a friend whose family used to play with the Ouija board. I wanted to use the board so I could contact my uncle, who had just passed away. My friend talked about how they would communicate with people who had passed away and were on the other side. Now this idea went against everything I believe in as a Christian. In fact, it was curiosity wrapped in danger. But before I could even make it to their home, my friend, not my parents, not my pastor, stepped in and wouldn't let me do it. I never even saw the board.

We currently live in an era where people don't share the same value system I grew up with. Everyone knows what they want because, after all, You Only Live Once (YOLO), right? However, the truth is that most people have a set of values, lines they will not cross. If you don't think you have them, you just haven't clearly established them yet. They are a guiding set of principles that you hold dear. Your values may align more toward family or work, but at the end of the day, they are the lines you will not cross.

Sometimes, God will use the people around you to hold you back from stepping over a line that you can't uncross. And sometimes, the thing that keeps you going is not a lack of mistakes, it's knowing which mistakes you're not willing to make. Over time, I've discovered the values that anchored my life: 1. My faith in God: My faith is the foundation for everything else. 2. The importance of a woman taking care of her husband: From Proverbs, I believe a woman should honor and care for her husband. 3. The Golden Rule: Treat others the way you want to be treated. It is the simplest way to stay compassionate, and it is probably one of the biggest reasons I am highly empathetic and discerning. 4. Self-sufficiency: Have your own, build your own. and 5. Authenticity: To thine own self be true, even when it's unpopular.

Let's be honest, all of that, values... sounds good on paper. But in life? They get tested. For me, the most significant clashes happen with family. I try to be as kind and non-judgmental as possible, but when I set a boundary that they've never seen from me before, it can cause conflict. People who are used to unlimited access don't take "no" well, especially when it is wrapped in kindness. But that's the point of a value: you don't hold it only when it's convenient. You hold it when it's tested.

One thing I've learned is that there is a difference between a value and a preference. Value is a guiding principle. It's solid, something you're not willing to bend for convenience. A preference is a choice or opinion that can shift based on relationships, proximity, or even one's mood. Knowing the difference is important because preferences can change without shaking who you are. Values? They are the root system of your identity.

Remember, values aren't about being perfect. The reason I bring up values at the beginning of the book is that they serve as the guiding principles and anchors for you. You feel confident in the decisions you make when they align with your values. What about when they don't? What about when your values change because life hits and hits hard?

When you live life doing things that go against your values, you have a value disconnect. This disconnect can leave you exhausted and mentally drained because you are constantly making choices and living a life that is not true to what you believe. When you show up in the world every day pretending like you're happy and that everything is good when it isn't, you are constantly allowing the enemy to steal a peace (that was purposeful) of your soul. I am here today to tell you to stop pretending.

You are doing everything you can just to show up in the world. Energy boosters, wild sex, drugs, or gossip, whatever you can think of that will numb the pain of what you truly feel. You have done it for so long that it feels natural to you; you think this is a part of who you are and who you were meant to be. But I challenge you today. I challenge you to be real and honest with yourself. Is it really who you are, or are you masking a deeper pain that you don't want to talk about or share?

Sometimes, when your values and your actions are not aligned, you end up in a pattern of overthinking. You think you are keeping the peace, but in reality, you are settling for less than you deserve. That is why your brain will not stop going, and why you continually overthink. You mentally create elaborate scenarios because deep down, something feels off. Your mind is trying to reason as to why we are in this situation. What is happening? It is signaling to you something is off, danger, check this out, but you keep going forward because you think it is the best course of action. That mental chaos you are experiencing is your value system trying to get your attention. It's your internal alarm system going off.

Another way to determine if your values may be misaligned is if you constantly find yourself saying, "Where are my people?" If you think you keep attracting people who drain, use, and take from you, then you aren't being true to your values. What you are doing is sending out a vibe, vibration, frequency to others who are also disconnected or prey on people who are disconnected. You are a magnet for people who need you to stay small because once you align with your path and purpose, once you realize your power and strength, you will outgrow your old surroundings exponentially.

Your body will also let you know when you are out of alignment. When you start getting those mysterious headaches, insomnia, and knots in your stomach every time you get a break. Your body is speaking the truth, even though your mind wants to lie. It is rebelling because it knows your truth. Your heart and mind are not connected. Stop lying to yourself. The next time you experience this, ask yourself this question: "What am I lying to myself about?"

When you go against your values time and again, your mind doesn't trust you, and it will erode your self-trust. You will find yourself staying quiet when you should speak up, or second-guessing every decision, or not even trusting your own decisions and needing validation from others before you feel confident about the choices you make. Do you wonder why you keep getting stuck in the same pattern? You have created an invisible ceiling when you are not true to yourself. You hit that invisible ceiling every time you try to be successful or go beyond where you are. Your mind thinks you are betraying yourself when you do, and you unconsciously self-sabotage because you are afraid of being seen.

In the end, what ends up happening is that you no longer recognize the person staring back at you in the mirror. You have been told things for so long that you think they are what you believe and who you are. You don't recognize yourself. You know exactly what everyone else needs and expects, but you couldn't tell anyone your expectations if your life depended on it. But here's the thing: Your life does depend on it. You have died internally and no longer recognize the person you see before you, but now you're tired of living this lie and have finally decided to choose yourself.

Chapter Two

Who Are You

Knowing your values gives you a compass. But a compass only matters if you know who's holding it. It's one thing to know what you believe in, it's another to know the person those beliefs belong to. Values and identity are deeply intertwined. Our values shape our choices, and our choices shape the way we see ourselves.

Trauma can rattle that connection. It can leave you staring in the mirror, wondering if the person looking back at you is still you or just a shell of you shaped by pain. And that leads to one of the most challenging and personal questions you can be asked after a life-altering experience: Who am I?

Who am I? This question is one of the most challenging and personal questions we get asked, and after trauma, it can feel impossible to answer. In this chapter, I want to explore with you what identity means and how it changes in response to life's most challenging moments and questions. We will explore how to begin piecing together a new sense of self in the wake of those experiences.

In my book Getting Over It, I talk about identifying your "It", that one thing that you need to get over. I believe that to deal with or move past things, we must identify the cause, the reason you are who or how you are. In this book, I want to first look at how you see yourself. Who do you say you are versus who others say that you are? Often, we perceive ourselves differently from how others view us. I believe that is because we know our internal thoughts and struggles, the ones we don't share with others, the ones that sometimes cause us to have a distorted world and self-view.

To get to the root or bottom of who we say we are, we have to peel the onion. There are layers to getting to the root of something. Our identity is a combination of personality traits, experiences, beliefs, values, and various roles that we may hold. Our identity isn't just the values or beliefs we have adopted for ourselves on our journey, but also those roles that society, family, or our culture says that we should hold. To this already multifaceted identity, we add job titles, relationship titles, statuses, personality traits, and hobbies. All of these items are intrinsically pieced together to bring the culmination of who you are, or who you still believe you are, or need to be as a person. Trauma, however, blows all of that up and leaves the roles, titles, personality traits, and whatever we hold dear scattered and shattered into shards we aren't able to identify. We then begin to question who we are after the pain.

I remember being asked this very question many years ago after undergoing severe trauma. In my neighborhood, there was a main strip where most people in my community congregated. One day, my sister wanted to introduce me to an older black Muslim gentleman who was friends with her best friend's family. The gentleman owned a store that sold items such as T-shirts and various other merchandise. Once introduced, I was fascinated by his perspectives on life and the wisdom he seemed to hold. At the time, I was in such a dark place and was also very ashamed of my appearance. I didn't have the same friendship relationships I had when I moved away, and I felt very alone and isolated in a town where almost everywhere I went, someone knew my name.

After the initial conversation, I would visit his shop daily. I would sit there for hours just talking and listening. At the time, it was just what I needed. One day, as we sat there talking and pondering the questions of life and what is right or wrong spiritually, he asked me the question that changed my life forever.

He began to speak in the slow baritone voice that he had... "My dear, who do you say you are?" I tilted my head slightly as I asked him questioningly, " What?' and he slowly repeated the question..." Who are you?"

I then began reciting my name and titles. The older gentleman immediately stopped me and stated, "No, beloved, not your name or what you do... but who.. my dear... are you?"

Stunned by the fact that he cut me off. Slightly taken aback because he had the audacity to assume I didn't comprehend such a fundamental question as Who are you? I jerked my head slightly and looked at him as he continued his question. I then took away the emotion and began to look within myself for the answers to that question. I had to ask myself, "Who are you, Jackie? What are the things about you that never changed? What is at the core of who you are? What are the things that I do naturally, not coaxed or prodded? I searched my mind for several minutes as he waited patiently for my answer. For several minutes, I thought back over my life to find the answers to that question.

I used the answer to that question to help bring me back to a place of peace. That answer helped me to reframe the negative self-image I had built of myself because of my appearance...because of my trauma. I would meditate on this answer daily. I read it aloud to myself while looking in the mirror daily to remind myself of who I am!!!!

If I asked you, 'Who are you?' what would your answer be? Would you give me a title? Would you give your name, your role, or your degree? The answers you provide are because of the place your answer holds in your life. We define ourselves by the importance we or society places on our identity traits. The more weight a title or role has, the more important it becomes.

Did you answer the question? If you answered the question, how much of who you said you are is shaped by your past experiences? Your future hopes? Are you basing who you are or who you want to be on expectations placed on you by others? Do you want to get married only because you keep getting asked when you will tie the knot? Or do you really want to be married? Do you find yourself fighting something you want to do, but feel the struggle because you're expected to do something different? For example, are you expected to stay married to an abusive spouse because your family does not believe in divorce? Are you expected to be a housewife? Who expects you to meet these standards? Is it cultural, societal, or familial? When you do what someone else expects, do you feel fulfilled, or do you feel like you're living someone else's life, or life for someone else?

Let me give you an example. Sarah had spent most of her life walking the tightrope of being a good girl. She knew what was expected of her: be polite, stay quiet, and live by the golden rule. But inside, it was a whole different story. Sarah had this fiery side she kept locked away: blunt, aggressive, and sometimes a little selfish. She wasn't proud of it because her parents, mainly her mother, often scolded her about being polite and commanding that she live by the Golden Rule... but she also couldn't deny it was there. She would end up in trouble whenever she let a glimpse of that side of her out. At home, she faced harsh discipline. Outside, her boldness often landed her in arguments, sometimes even fights, battles she wasn't equipped to win. So, she figured the safest move was to bury that part of herself and keep it hidden so that only those closest to her would even know it existed.

For years, Sarah played the role of the quiet, people-pleasing doormat, bending over backwards to make everyone happy. But that internal battle didn't just disappear. It bubbled under the surface, morphing into passive aggressiveness and simmering resentment. Deep down, Sarah wanted to unleash her inner assertiveness, but her fear of rejection and of failing to meet everyone's expectations kept her stuck. She was convinced that she could not be true to herself and please others.

Then, one day, everything changed. Sarah started experiencing sharp pain and stomach issues, which led to a doctor's visit and the diagnosis of ulcers. The stress of constantly suppressing her true self was eating away at her. That was the breaking point. One day, without warning, she snapped. Years of bottled-up frustration came pouring out in a wave of unfiltered aggression. For a moment, she felt a mix of freedom and terror. This wasn't the solution she wanted, but it was a wake-up call she needed.

Determined to get to the root of it all, Sarah sought the help of a therapist. First, it was hard to open up. Sarah had been down the therapy road before, and it hadn't helped. The previous therapists did not make her feel comfortable or even safe to open up and share. How could she admit that the good girl everyone knew was someone else entirely? Session by session, Sarah began peeling back the layers of her beliefs. She realized that the voice telling her she had to be perfect, quiet, and self-sacrificing wasn't hers. This voice had been drilled into her as a child. The words were not even spoken, but it is how she interpreted them. Those expectations weren't truths; they were limiting beliefs, and as she examined them, she realized how much they had held her back.

Sarah experienced a moment of identity crisis. Why was this a crisis? The thing that Sarah wanted to do was in contrast to what she was told that her identity should be. She was in a constant state of confusion and chaos internally because she rarely ever spoke up to protect herself or voice her opinion. She thought speaking up in defense of yourself meant keeping quiet, pretending to be ok with situations and circumstances, when you really want more. Sarah learned this behavior...she patterned herself after the one who taught her...her mother. How do you combat that?

Unstoppable: A 5 step Guide to Reclaiming Identity & Purpose

Now that we have examined one of Sarah's moments of identity crisis, let's delve deeper into determining if you are currently experiencing an identity crisis. Let's look at who you are inside, not in terms of roles or titles, but at the essence of your being. What is at the core of your being? What is the essence of who you are? What things about you have never changed, that you value and protect with everything in you? They could be kindness, sincerity, integrity, or any number of things. Again, I ask, "Who are you?"

Are you the person who goes along to get along? Are you a rule breaker? Are you intelligent? Do you try your best to fit in so you don't stick out like a sore thumb? Are you making sure you color between the lines because you fear being ostracized or picked on by others? When you're around others, do you feel like you're being true to who you are, or are you a chameleon being all things to all people, but never being true to yourself? Are you truly a hospitable southern belle who minds her manners, or are you pretending to be so that you can fit in?

Let's look at your answer to the question. When you answered the question, who did you say you were? Were you a title or role? Did your past, present, or future shape your answer?

Let's revisit Sarah, a young woman on a journey of self-discovery. When someone asked, 'Who are you?' Sarah would confidently answer, 'I'm a loving and kind woman who cares deeply about people. While this is true, it wasn't the whole story. Deep down, Sarah knew there was more to her identity than what she could articulate, but she wasn't sure how to uncover it. Her response, though heartfelt, felt like a safe and practiced version of herself rather than the complete picture of who she truly was.

Determined to understand herself better, Sarah decided to dig deeper. Therapy became her starting point, a safe space to ask herself the hard questions and confront the truths she had been avoiding. It was not easy, but Sarah learned to be honest with herself in a way she hadn't been before. She began to peel back the layers of her personality, examining her actions and motivations, fears, and patterns. This process reveals a more complex and vibrant person than she had ever realized.

Through this journey, Sarah discovered that her kindness and love for people were only part of her story. She also learned that she had a strong desire to help others in meaningful ways, but that didn't mean she had to sacrifice herself in the process. Sarah recognized her need to set boundaries, something she had always struggled with, and found that being assertive was not a betrayal of her kindness but an extension of it. She began to see that loving herself and protecting her energy made her ability to love others even stronger.

As Sarah explored the core of her thoughts and the essence of her being, she found answers she didn't know she was looking for. She realized that her identity wasn't limited to the qualities that others admired about her or the roles she played in their lives. It was about her values, dreams, and the person she was becoming. Sarah's journey was far from over, but she had taken the first critical steps in reclaiming her full, authentic self. This journey of self-discovery wasn't just about finding answers; it was about becoming someone who no longer needed to fit neatly into one description but who could embrace the multifaceted, ever-evolving person she truly was.

Now ask yourself: "Am I doing what truly makes me happy, or am I always trying to please other people? If you remove cultural and societal expectations, what is it that you truly want? Who are you at the core? These questions may seem easy, but they aren't, and the answers when you truly dig deep will be uncomfortable. Sometimes, we hold on to certain beliefs or ways of being because they're tied to people we care about or ideals we don't want to challenge. I've been there. Some parts of me haven't changed because I don't want to disappoint my dad.

I remember a recent conversation with my Dad where he said, "If it was good enough for my dad, it's good enough for me." At first, I thought that it was literal, but the truth is more nuanced. My dad always encouraged me to stand for what I believe. He seems proud of the fact that I sometimes challenge the norm, and he knows that his daughters have grown into strong, independent women. His words, layered with both tradition and encouragement, remind me how complex our foundations can be... shaped by love, culture, and sometimes fear of disappointing others.

When you start to search for the core of who you are, look at the foundation on which you built your decision, what are the values you hold sacred, the lines you won't cross, and the causes you feel compelled to stand up for? Who are you now at this moment? And as you ask yourself these questions, is your identity shaped by truth, trauma, or tradition, or perhaps a mix of all three? Understanding your core requires peeling the layers to reveal the fundamental essence of who you are.

Let's talk about your core. What is your core? Your core is your deepest part, the essence of your identity. It's where your values, beliefs, motivations, and authentic self reside. It's not about the roles you play or the labels you've been given; it's about what drives you, what fuels your emotions, and shapes your perspectives on life. Your core is where your truest truths live, and understanding this is a vital step toward personal growth, self-discovery, and living an authentic life.

Remember, this is also a journey of self-discovery and understanding, not about perfection. When you know the essence of who you are, you can make decisions with confidence, resilience, and purpose. It's an act of reclaiming your identity and creating a life that truly reflects your values and aspirations.

Meet Elena. She was a 29-year-old teacher with a natural gift for connecting with people. On the outside, she seemed content: her friends admired her kindness, her students adored her, and her family was proud of the steady life she built. But on the inside, Elena felt stuck. She couldn't quite explain it, so she had this nagging feeling that something was missing. When people asked her about herself, she always replied, I'm a teacher, and I love helping kids. While true, it didn't feel like the whole picture. Deep down, Elena wondered if she really knew herself at all.

Elena decided to dig deeper, starting with the question that felt both simple and overwhelming: Am I living the life I want, or am I living to make everyone else happy? She realized that much of her identity had been shaped by the expectations of others, her parents, pride in her career, her friends' admiration for her reliability, and her students' trust in her guidance. She loved those roles, but were they her? Was she living authentically, or was she holding onto a version of herself that fit a mold? The thought both excited and terrified her.

One evening, Elena called her mom to talk after a tough day at work. "Do you think I've made the right choices in my life?" She asked hesitantly. Her mom paused and replied, "You've always made us proud. You're like your father: steady and responsible. If it was good enough for us, it is good enough for you." Elena was taken aback. Her mom meant well, but those words only amplified her doubts. Was she following a path out of tradition, and the need for approval, or something she genuinely wanted? Memories of her dad, who recently passed away (a man who had always encouraged her to think for herself) surfaced in her mind. He had once said, "Sometimes somebody's feelings will be hurt. Better theirs than yours."

Elena later decided to explore what her core beliefs really were. She began journaling daily, asking herself questions like: What truly makes me happy? And what do I stand for? She noticed that while she loved teaching, her real passion lay in empowering others. She wanted to help her students and adults like herself, people searching for meaning and direction. She realized that her foundation was strong, built on kindness and love, but it had cracks shaped by her fear of disappointing others. She needed to patch those cracks with honesty and courage to pursue what mattered to her.

Elena began to reclaim her identity through therapy, mindfulness, and reflection. She began to set boundaries and allowed herself to say no without feeling guilty. She began to reframe her relationship and career by choosing to view them as stepping stones to her larger dream of becoming a life coach and helping others on a broader scale. She realized she wasn't abandoning who she was or her life experiences but rather building on them. She began to align her actions with what mattered to her. For the first time in her life, she felt that her decisions reflected her values, needs, wants, and desires, and not just the expectations of others.

Elena's journey wasn't easy, but it was liberating. She learned that understanding her core was not about rejecting her past, but about embracing her true self, her foundation, which included kindness, love, and resilience, that had always been there. By digging deep, she uncovered the strength to rebuild and expand on who she was, creating a life that felt more authentic and full of possibility. And when someone asked Who are you... she now answered with a smile and confidence that she hadn't known before: I'm Elena, and I'm building the life I was meant to live.

I am telling Elena's story to highlight the importance of understanding your core and foundation. I want you to see what happens when your core beliefs and thoughts are challenged by loss, uncertainty, or a life-altering event. It is in those moments that we are forced to confront who we are. In the process of disruption and rebuilding, we discover things about ourselves that we never realized were there.

Trauma just hits differently, and when it happens, it severs our connection to the familiar. It reveals just how fragile life can be. Suddenly, those roles and titles we once took pride in can feel empty or distant. Our beliefs and values feel shaken, and we begin to question everything and every part of ourselves. The parts of us that used to define us: our work ethic, passions, routines, and even our confidence, may feel distant or irrelevant, as if they belong to someone else entirely. It can even make us feel indifferent towards the things and people we love.

This loss of connection is one of trauma's most painful things, leaving us feeling empty. It is, however, normal to feel disoriented and grieve the loss of that part of you that is now missing. There is a silver lining: the disruption gives us a chance to strip away the loads we carry out of habit or expectation and ask ourselves, what parts of me are truly me? Trauma's aftermath is painful, but it can also be the beginning of a deeper understanding, helping us define or redefine who we are from a place of truth rather than tradition.

On this new journey of self-discovery, you're going to have to peel back the layers of who you used to be and understand what is still true about you today after the pain. This journey may feel intense and strange. It will take some introspection, asking yourself Who am I today? What do I believe? What values do I still hold dear? What I used to think is no longer valid based on the experiences I have gone through. People who experience racism, who have never experienced it before, change their beliefs after the experience. Someone who was robbed by someone who they never thought would be capable of such a thing often changes their beliefs and sometimes values after their traumatic experience. Someone who loses a child may stop or start believing in God. Trauma and life experiences have a way of changing people. I know I have changed many people's views of African Americans by taking the time to answer questions they had about why black people do the things they do. Trauma has a way of separating everything we consider significant, allowing us to see what really matters. As they say, "Life be Lifing!"

This reflection can be surprisingly freeing. You don't have to keep dragging around parts of yourself that you've outgrown or never even connected with. This is the chance to explore the values that feel genuine and true: whether it's compassion, creativity, resilience, or the need for inner peace. These values will become an anchor, something we hold on to even when everything else feels shaky. As we focus on these core values, we will begin to see a new, more grounded version of ourselves. We're no longer living by default or on autopilot; instead, we are choosing what defines us from a place of authenticity. It's not about clinging to the past or rebuilding exactly what we had: it's about finding a way forward that feels aligned with who you are today.

Sometimes, letting go of the parts of you that no longer fit can be the most liberating part of healing after trauma. Why, because we hold on to those old, outdated views that weigh us down and are contrary to what we feel or believe. We think those were the things that gave us a sense of purpose, not realizing that many times it was the weight that was holding us down. As we examine our lives, we learn how many things we did to make other people happy with us, to meet the expectations of others, or because it was where we felt safe.

Letting go may feel like a loss, like grieving someone you knew well. It will take time and self-compassion to accept that who you are today may look completely different than the person you were yesterday. This is another reason why it is crucial that, after a relationship loss, you take time to self-reflect so you don't attract the same type of person and to ensure you are healed and okay. You don't want to take the pain and loss from one relationship to another.

Remember, as you let go of the old, you allow new pieces of you to be released. These parts can be accepted with joy because you have chosen to make them a part of your life and not something you were told you had to because of culture or society. You may begin to feel lighter, less bound, and freer to explore what truly brings you joy and fulfillment at this new phase of your life. This doesn't mean you are rejecting your past; it means you're making room for a future that reflects who you are today, not who you felt you had to be. As you let go, you will find a new kind of freedom that is rooted in choice and self-acceptance. Instead of clinging to who you used to be, you can start building a life that feels real and right in the present moment, allowing yourself to evolve without judgment.

One of my favorite Bible scriptures says, "But be ye transformed by the renewing of your mind." Building a new identity after trauma is like starting with a blank slate. It is like being transformed with a renewed mind. It is both exciting and terrifying because this time, you're choosing what defines you. You get to decide what parts of our past you want to keep, which passions to reignite, and what new dreams and goals align with who you are becoming. This journey doesn't happen overnight; It's a gradual process of discovery, and it's OK if you don't have all the answers. Instead of feeling pressure to get it right, you can approach this as an opportunity to experiment, explore, and try out what feels meaningful at this moment. We're not trying to fit back into who we used to be; we're creating something new that feels true and aligns with our present selves.

What's great about this process is that it gives you permission to change and evolve. There's no need to lock yourself into a rigid definition of who you are. Your new identity can be flexible, fluid, and adaptable as you grow. You might discover new interests, develop fresh perspectives, or find strength in areas we didn't know you had. It's about building a self that is resilient, adaptable, and uniquely your own. It will be shaped by everything you've been through, but not defined by it. I want you to catch that: **"YOU** will **NOT** be **defined** by what you've gone through." This is not about forgetting the past or erasing what happens; it's about choosing what you carry forward and letting yourself grow into a version of yourself that feels whole and true. Live life on your own terms, embrace the freedom to define who you are, and know that you have the strength to keep evolving as you move forward.

CHAPTER THREE:

THE FIGHT

Once you begin to uncover who you are at the core, beyond titles, roles, and other people's expectations, you quickly realize that identity isn't rebuilt in peace and comfort. It's built in conflict. The moment trauma or loss hits, your values and your identity collide with fear, confusion, and survival instincts. That's when you step into what I call the fight phase. This isn't just about fighting external battles; it's about the war we fight within, the fight to hold onto yourself when everything familiar has been shaken.

And now we meet Shondra and Jessica.

Shondra and Jake had built what many would call the perfect life. For 25 years, they had been a power couple, raising two children and carving out a home in one of Georgia's most sought-after neighborhoods. Their home was a spacious, sunlit colonial with immaculate landscape, and it was the center of countless happy memories. Inside, Shondra ran her home with grace. She was a stay-at-home mom by choice, and she poured herself into her family. Every morning, she would get up and ensure her children were fed and ready for school before turning her attention to her teacup Yorkie named Angel, a tiny ball of sandy brown and black fur who was pampered almost as much as the children. Angel was groomed weekly by a top-notch trainer and was a reflection of Shondra's impeccable taste and attention to detail.

Shondra took pride in how she presented her family. Jake, her husband, an investment banker with a natural charm and razor-sharp mind, had always been her biggest cheerleader. From day one, he showered her with affection, gifts, and unwavering support. Shondra had everything she thought she wanted: designer clothes, extravagant vacations, and a husband who loved to spoil her. Her days were full of purpose: managing the household, keeping the kids on track, staying up-to-date with the latest trends, and still finding time to prepare home-cooked meals. She worked tirelessly to make Jake look and feel like the King of his castle. In her mind, their life was a dream come true.

But as time passed, cracks began to form in their seemingly perfect facade. The children grew up and left for college, leaving behind a quiet house and a mother struggling to find a new purpose. Shondra decided to pour her energy into Jake. He was her rock, her soul mate after all, the man she had built this life with. She thought this was the perfect opportunity to reconnect and rekindle their bond. Yet, Jake didn't seem to respond the way she expected. What Shondra didn't see, what she couldn't see, was that Jake was battling feelings of loneliness and neglect. While she had been busy ensuring the family looked flawless from the outside, Jake felt increasingly invisible. He craved intimacy, honesty, and connection, but instead, he felt like a piece in Shondra's carefully curated image.

Jake's frustration eventually led him down a path neither of them could have predicted. Lonely and unable to communicate how he felt, he formed an emotional connection with someone else. It wasn't planned, and it wasn't what he wanted, but in this other woman, he found someone who saw him, who listened without judgment. Jake realized he no longer felt at home in his marriage. Every time he wanted to talk to Shondra, she shut him down. Every time he wanted to go somewhere intimate, she shut him down.

Whenever he wanted to have a casual day out, she shut him down. Everything had to fit into Shondra's perfect little picture, and frankly, he was tired. The thought broke him, but he knew he had to tell Shondra the truth. He no longer wanted to only be intimate with his wife at scheduled times; he wanted spontaneity. He wanted his fun wife back in his life. He confessed over dinner one night, with shaking hands and a heavy heart, he told her about the other woman, his feelings of abandonment, and his decision to leave. Shondra was blindsided. Her world had fallen from under her as Jake, the man she had dedicated her life to, calmly told her there was no fixing the relationship. She begged to understand and to make things right, but Jake's answer was firm.

Her mind raced. As Shondra sat there, her knees were weak, and tears were streaming down her face. How had they gone wrong? How had the life she built with so much love and care unraveled in an instant? She thought she had been the perfect wife, the perfect mother. But now, she sat there questioning everything: her choices, priorities, and her very identity. And as Jake walked out of their home that evening, she realized her journey wasn't over; it was just beginning, but this time, it would be a path she would have to walk alone.

Let's look at another person: Jessica. Jessica's life had always revolved around her family. At 30, she was a stay-at-home wife with two young children, a devoted husband, and a carefully crafted life of love and routine. But her foundation, the core of who she was, had been shaped long before. Growing up, it was just Jessica, her two siblings, and their mother, Lisa. Lisa was a force of nature, a single mom who had taken on the world for her kids. She juggled two jobs, scraped together meals when money was tight, and still managed to be the warm, encouraging presence they needed. Jessica idolized her mom, seeing her as the ultimate example of strength and sacrifice.

Things weren't always easy, but Lisa never let her children feel the weight of her struggles. Eventually, after years of late nights and early mornings, Lisa earned her college degree, and their lives began to shift. The family moved into a better neighborhood, and life began to feel better. Then came Jared, the man Lisa would marry. He brought stability and laughter to their home, filling in some of the gap's life had carved out. Jessica adored him for how he loved her mother, but no one could ever take Lisa's place as her rock.

Life seemed to settle into a rhythm until it didn't. One day, Lisa began to feel off. At first, it was fatigue and aching pain that she couldn't shake. Jessica told her to see a doctor, but Lisa brushed it off. She was too busy and too important to her family to slow down. Then came the diagnosis: stage 4 breast cancer. It hit like a hurricane, sudden and merciless, and within two weeks, Lisa was gone. There was no time to prepare: just like that, Jessica's best friend, her cheerleader, her mom, was ripped from her life.

After Shondra's heartbreak and Jessica's loss of her mom, both women found themselves in the fight phase. Their stories may appear different, but their bodies and minds are responding in the same way, as if they are in danger. As each day passes, Shondra's mind races with questions. She fights each day to have cohesive thoughts, and as she questions everything, she eats less than she used to, trusts fewer people, and becomes increasingly paranoid, thinking that everyone is against her. Shondra did not realize until much later that she was spiraling downward... She had begun catastrophic thinking.

In Jessica's case, her thoughts won't stop. They raced through her mind, rapidly and relentlessly, as if each one demanded her full attention. Grief has a way of taking over like this, leaving you feeling untethered and vulnerable. People around her listen, offering sympathy, but they rarely challenge her thoughts: after all, who would argue with someone mourning the death of a loved one? Jessica goes through her days looking fine on the outside, but inside her mind is spiraling. Her thoughts would constantly spiral toward the worst-case scenarios, making every slight worry feel like an insurmountable crisis. She fights to get out of bed.

Whether it is grief or betrayal, the fight phase looks similar: thoughts that spiral out of control, emotions that won't stop, and bodies that think they are under attack. This is why it's important for you to understand your body's adrenal response. The adrenal glands flood our system with stress hormones such as adrenaline and cortisol, pushing us into survival mode. But what does that look like in the stories above?

Fight looks like Shondra replaying the betrayal repeatedly, trying to control every detail of her environment, becoming defensive, and even angry.

Flight might be Jessica throwing herself into busy work; anything to escape the pain she doesn't want to face.

Freeze shows up when you feel paralyzed, unable to make a decision, stuck in place while the world moves on without you.

Fawn (a lesser-known response) can be when someone wants to please others to avoid conflict or abandonment.

These aren't signs of weakness; they are the body's natural response to being in survival mode; they are biological survival strategies. Your brain and body is doing what it was designed to do: *keep you alive.* The problem is that when the crisis is over, your body doesn't always know how to shut it off. When it happens daily, there are damaging effects to our health, such as heart problems, anxiety and depression, hormonal imbalance, digestive issues, and countless other physical ailments. So when Shondra keeps asking *How did I get here?* Or *what are people saying about me?* Her body is stuck in fight mode. When Jessica feels like she has to hold it all together, she's running on adrenaline in flight mode.

Understanding this is crucial to healing because once you can name what your body is doing, you can teach it that you are safe, loved, and capable of moving forward.

In emergencies, these reactions are helpful, but in the long run, they take a toll on your body. Catastrophic thinking keeps you stuck in worst-case scenarios, Isolation convinces you that nobody understands, and exhaustion makes you feel powerless to keep going. So, the danger is not always trauma; it is the mental and emotional spiral that follows.

This is why you feel exhausted, foggy, or not yourself after prolonged stress. Your body is crying out for rest, not another surge of adrenaline. Healing means learning to pause, breathe, and give your body the safety signals it needs, instead of the constant stress signals. As they say on the airplanes: Put your mask on first.

Let's get back to Shondra.

After her divorce, Shondra was shattered. She couldn't understand how everything she had done (everything she thought a Good Wife was supposed to do) had failed to keep her husband's affections. How could it have come to this? Her mind raced with unanswered questions, and the thought of Jake falling in love with someone else was a knife twisting deeper into her heart. Desperate for closure, she called, texted, and emailed him, pleading for a chance to talk. For weeks, she was met with silence, but finally, Jake agreed to meet her at a local coffee shop.

When Shondra walked in, her appearance spoke volumes about the emotional turmoil she had endured. Her scarf was slightly askew, and dark sunglasses covered her eyes, swollen from countless hours of crying. Jake was already seated, a somber expression on his face, his hands clasped together as though bracing himself. As Shondra removed her sunglasses and sat down, tears welled up in her already red eyes. Jake reached across the table to grab her hand; his voice was heavy with compassion towards her. I never wanted to hurt you," he began, "but I couldn't keep living a lie. I wasn't happy anymore."

Shondra's voice trembled as she forced out the words, "How long? How long were you unhappy?" (She looked questioningly.)? "I don't understand. "We smiled; We took trips with the kids,..." I thought everything was OK." Her face was a mix of pain and longing, searching Jake's eyes for answers that might make sense of her devastation. Jake sighed; his tone measured but weary. "Yes, I smiled for the kids. I stayed at first, hoping things would change, hoping you would hear me. I tried to tell you what I needed, what I was missing. I wanted more than just a clean house and cared-for kids. I needed you."

He continued, his voice rising slightly with years of pent-up frustration. "Shondra, you were always so busy... cooking, cleaning, keeping the house running. By the end of the day, you were to tired to talk, let alone be intimate. I would suggest trips for just the two of us... Our children were old enough to stay home alone, but you wouldn't leave them. When I had a bad day at work, you didn't ask me how my day went or how I was doing. Your ears were always open to solving the problems for everyone but me. I began to feel like a burden. I felt like I had to be perfect to fit into your nicely woven picture frame. I tried Shondra for years. I pleaded for years."

Tears streamed down Shondra's face as she interrupted, her voice breaking. "But I was taking care of you... of the kids, the house. I thought that's what I was supposed to do as your wife." Jake's expression softened, but his resolve remained firm. "I needed more, and you didn't listen. I don't want to argue. I'm done. I have nothing left to talk about." He stood, placing a gentle but final hand on her shoulder. "I care about you, and I'll always love you in my own way. I hope you have a good life Shondra." Jake stood and walked out of the coffee shop, leaving Shondra frozen in place.

Her world imploded. Shondra's mind spiraled into chaos, consumed with questions, pain, and the weight of her upbringing. Everything she thought she was supposed to be, a beautiful wife, a nurturing mother, felt like a betrayal of herself. Her thoughts became a battlefield, waging war over her identity and her worth. Her body reacted as though under attack, plunging her into fight or flight mode, unable to distinguish between emotional devastation and the physical threats. Shondra's journey into the depths of her despair was only beginning, but in this pain lay the faintest whisper of something more: a chance to confront the essence of who she was and who she would become.

Part of this fight involves peeling back layers of yourself to examine what lies underneath. You might realize that certain aspects of your old identity weren't as fulfilling as you thought or that you've been holding on to beliefs that no longer serve you. Like Shondra's idea of a good wife, the revelation of these discoveries can be uncomfortable, even painful, but they are also freeing. They allow you to identify what's worth keeping and let go of what no longer fits, guiding you closer to an identity that feels true to who you are now. This process isn't about erasing the past; it's about evolving into the most authentic version of yourself.

Shondra realized she had to rebuild and rebuilding your identity can feel like stepping into an intense, personal battle to reclaim the pieces of yourself that seem lost. There is no straightforward map for this process, no universal guide to what comes next. It's uncharted territory, filled with emotions and questions you might have avoided for years. This journey forces you to confront your pain, frustration, and confusion head-on, which can be both terrifying and transformative. It requires a deep well of courage to begin the fight and even more resilience to keep going when the road feels overwhelming. But the rewards of reclaiming yourself are worth every single moment of the struggle.

Shondra eventually realized that she wasn't just grieving her marriage, she was grieving who she was in that identity that kept her feeling safe. Jessica discovered that even her strength, learned from her mother, had cracks when grief ripped away her foundation. Both women, like many of us, learned that the fight isn't about protecting an image or clinging to old roles. It is about rebuilding a version of ourselves that's authentic, resilient, and whole.

Rebuilding will feel messy, and some days you will feel stronger than others. That doesn't mean you are failing. It means you're fighting. Every tear, every journal entry, every moment of self-compassion is a step forward. The fight isn't a sprint. It's a marathon. It's about pacing yourself, resting when you need to, and refusing to give up on the possibility of becoming whole again.

CHAPTER 4

BUT AM I THOUGH?

You've discovered that while you are in the fight phase, you experience mental, emotional, and physical trauma to your body. These changes are usually invisible to the naked eye, and unless you tell someone, they may not know what is happening to you. Trauma doesn't only live in your memories; it shows up in your body. Stress can alter your sleep, appetite, energy levels, and even impact your overall health. Most of it goes unseen. To others, they see the person they've always seen. They don't see you as a person who is internally kicking themselves, second-guessing every step, questioning your worth, and silently battling to hold it all together. This leaves you feeling misunderstood or invisible.

This disparity often occurs because people can only see what's on the surface; they notice how you present yourself in the world, your smile, your accomplishments, and your daily routine, but they can't see the inner turmoil you're navigating. You have learned how to hide your true feelings very well, and after a traumatic event, you might feel like you're walking around with a giant neon sign that says I'm struggling, but the truth is, many people don't even notice the subtle changes. And even if they do, they may not know how to respond. Meanwhile, you're left feeling disconnected, and the person everyone thinks you are is a stranger to you now.

What makes this even more challenging is that trauma often

distorts your self-perception. It's like looking at yourself through a funhouse mirror, except it's not fun. You begin to question everything: your strengths, your worth, even your identity. You might focus on the ways you think you failed or the things that you've lost, while others are still looking at your achievements and positive traits. This disconnect is so isolating that it makes bridging the gap between your internal reality and the external world even harder.

The good news is that this disconnect doesn't have to be permanent. Part of the healing process is learning to rebuild your sense of self, not based on who you used to be or how others see you, but on who you are now. It's about closing the gap between the internal and external, finding ways to share your struggles with those you trust, and permitting yourself to grow into a new version of yourself. It's a process, and like any process, it takes time, but it's also an opportunity to rediscover your strengths and reshape how you see yourself moving forward.

Let's talk about Shondra.

Shondra sat in her living room, staring blankly at the sunlight filtering through the blinds. To anyone looking in, she still appeared every bit as stunning and successful as she had always been. Her makeup was flawless, her hair was effortlessly styled, and she wore her signature elegance like armor. Yet, inside, she felt like a shattered version of herself. Whenever someone called her beautiful or strong, it felt like a cruel joke, like they were describing someone else entirely. She thought they were making fun of her, and she wanted to scream, "But am I"? Because she certainly didn't feel like it.

Shondra's Mind churned relentlessly, replaying every detail of the past few months since her divorce from Jake. The whispers of pity and the casual way her friends glossed over her pain with words like "you're better off without him" only made her feel more isolated. Did they even know what she was going through? Did they see how she flinched at her reflection and questioned every choice she had made over the last 10 years? Shondra didn't trust their reassurances. A more profound, darker thought gnawed at her: *What if they knew? What if they knew Jake was cheating and said nothing?*

With that one thought, Shondra began pulling away from everyone, friends, family, and anyone they knew. The people she once leaned on now felt like strangers. Their compliments rang hollow, their conversations shallow. "You're so strong," Shondra they say, or "You're going to come out of this better than ever," **But am I**? She wondered each time, her mind quick to refute every kind word with her own harsh judgment. I'm not strong, I'm a failure, I'm not beautiful, and I wasn't even enough for my husband. The overthinking was relentless, and the more she questioned herself, the harder it became to believe anyone's sincerity.

Shondra avoided invitations, declined calls, and dodged people in public. Even at the grocery store, she would peek around aisles, ducking out of sight if she spotted someone she knew. She didn't want to hear one more person say it would get better or see the looks of pity on their faces. After all, she has too much pride for that. Her world grew smaller by the day, confined to the four walls of her apartment. There, she didn't have to perform; she could slip and feel the raw weight of her pain. Yet even in solitude, the questions haunted her: *Why didn't Jake love me enough? What did I do wrong? Was I really so blind?*

In spite of her attempts to shut the world out, the occasional text or voicemail would pierce through. Her best friend Monica had left one just the day before: "Shondra, please call me back. I'm worried about you. You are amazing and don't deserve to go through this alone." Shondra stared at the message. Her chest began to tighten, and she asked herself: But am I? She thought again, she couldn't bring herself to believe Monica's words; what if Monica didn't mean them? What if she only pitied her? What if, worst of all, Monica had seen the cracks in her marriage long before and didn't say anything?

Shondra's days blurred together; her isolation feeding her insecurities and vice versa. Yet deep down on the inside, a tiny part of her whispered that this wasn't who she was meant to be. That part of her, buried deep under layers of doubt and pain, wondered if she could ever rebuild herself, not as the person others thought she was, but as the person she wanted to be. For now, though, she remained trapped in her own mind, questioning everything, especially herself.

As we've learned, crises and fight phases don't happen overnight; instead, they develop slowly over time, and Shondra gradually transformed into a different person. A person who built a wall of defense to protect herself from the pain. A prideful person who didn't want to share their pain with those who truly cared and genuinely wanted to help. A person who believes everyone is against them, so they have to protect themselves. A person who becomes highly empathetic because their survival depends on picking up the emotions and pain of others.

When you have moments or areas where you think this isn't who I am, know that you may be in a crisis. This is a moment you find yourself doing something that goes against what you believe. Why are you allowing this moment to continue? What is keeping you bound or tied to this thing or thought that has a strong hold on you and your thoughts? Where does the root originate, and how did it grow? Once you find it, ask yourself why and keep asking until you get to the root of the issue. At the root, you may find bitterness, resentment, or some other emotion or core belief, and once you find it, you can address and make the necessary adjustments to remove or reframe the root of the issue.

How do you get rid of the root? First, let me say that I found a helpful tool that helped me when I was trying to identify the root of some of my own emotions. It is an emotion Wheel. I would use it to determine my current emotion and follow the feeling to uncover the root cause. For example, if I were feeling sad, I would look at the sub root, which may have been guilt, and the real issue I had was one of two things: remorse or shame. I would then determine which one and ask myself why until I got to the root of the problem, and usually, I would feel so much better. It may not be as easy for everyone, but I couldn't always afford a therapy session.

Let's look at Jane.

Jane had always set a rule for herself regarding relationships, two years that was her limit for deciding whether to stay or go. If things weren't moving forward or didn't feel right, she would move on. But here she is, five years into her relationship with Charles, and asking herself the one question she thought she'd never need to ask: Why am I still here? The thought caught her off guard, and she spiraled into an internal dialogue that refused to be ignored.

Because I love him, she told herself. But that answer felt too simple, too rehearsed. OK, Jane, she thought, but why do you love him? The answer bubbled up easily enough: because he makes me feel loved and wanted. That felt more honest, but it still wasn't the whole story. She kept digging, asking herself, How does he make you feel loved and wanted? What does he do, that's different?

Her mind was flooded with memories. She thought about how Charles cherished every inch of her when they made love, as if she were the most beautiful thing he had ever seen. She remembered the romantic text messages he would send her during the day, simple, thoughtful notes that always seemed to come at just the right time. Then there were the nights when he would sense her stress without her saying a word, and he knew exactly what she needed. A glass of wine, a warm bath, her favorite book on her tray, and dinner already taken care of, he made her feel seen, truly seen, in a way she had never experienced before.

Why does this matter so much to me? Jane wondered. The answer hit her like a wave: Because I've never felt this way before. Her feelings and desires had always been an afterthought throughout her life and in her past relationships. No one had ever gone out of their way to make her feel appreciated or prioritized, but with Charles, it was different. He didn't tell her she mattered; he showed her in ways that felt undeniable, ways that made her feel like she was the center of his world.

As Jane sat with these thoughts, she realized something deeper about herself. The reason she was still here wasn't just about Charles; it was about her. For the first time, she allowed herself to feel worthy of the kind of love she had always wanted but never dared to expect. Charles wasn't just a partner; He was the person who helped her see what it meant to feel valued, and at that moment, she began to understand why she stayed. It wasn't just love: It was transformation.

Here is the crux of her conflict: It is believed that if a man dates you for years, he doesn't really want to be married to you; he is only there out of convenience or necessity. Although her actual situation says he loves me, he is just going through some trying times right now, and that is what she wants to believe.

At first, Jane didn't fully understand how much her past had shaped her core beliefs. The two-year rule was more about protecting herself from rejection or being taken for granted. At her core, she believed that if she or her boyfriend didn't decide to get married or take steps towards it, then the relationship was a waste of time. With Charles, those concerns seemed to dissipate. His consistent efforts to show her love challenged the belief that it was a waste of time to stay in the relationship for an extended period. For Jane, staying with Charles wasn't just about him; it was about permitting herself to experience love in a way that felt safe, healing, and affirming.

Yet, there was an internal conflict. Jane often wondered if staying with Charles meant she was compromising her values or betraying her promise to herself. But when she reflected on what this relationship gave her —emotional growth, validation, and a sense of being cherished —she realized it wasn't about abandoning her beliefs. Instead, it was about evolving them. She understood that core beliefs aren't rigid rules, but rather frameworks that can grow and change as we do. In Charles, Jane found more than love; she found a partner who helped her verbalize what truly mattered to her.

But let's talk about how it was so easy for Jane to ignore her wants and desires. Jane had a knack for tolerating things that most people wouldn't. It wasn't that she lacked self-respect or didn't know what she deserved; it was more that she had grown so accustomed to adapting. This is something she learned as a coping mechanism. It never seemed to matter whether she liked something or someone, because her thoughts and desires seemed insignificant to everyone but her. This tolerance manifested in subtle ways in her relationship with Charles, but it was perhaps most apparent when he dodged her hints about marriage. Despite his declarations of love and devotion, every time the subject of marriage came up, he'd find a way to deflect or delay. And while it stung, Jane let it slide. Why? Because she was used to it.

For most of Jane's life, she had learned to live with people giving her the bare minimum. They'd do enough to satisfy her but not make her feel truly fulfilled. It started when she was young, family members who made promises they didn't keep, friends who only showed up when it was convenient for them, and past relationships where her needs were an afterthought. Over time, Jane had internalized the idea that her desires were secondary and that she should be grateful if someone gave her just enough. Charles loved her, that she was sure, but his hesitation on marriage was one more example of a familiar pattern: people meeting her needs on their terms, not hers.

What made Jane stick around wasn't blind devotion; it was her ability to adapt. She had grown skilled at finding the silver lining in situations others might find unacceptable. Yes, Charles hadn't proposed, but he was still thoughtful, attentive, and loving in ways that felt meaningful. To Jane, his actions proved that he cared, even if his reluctance to commit frustrated her. She rationalized that no one was perfect and that focusing on the good in their relationship was better than focusing on what was missing. This mindset had carried her through various relationships before Charles, and it became a survival mechanism she relied on.

But deep down, Jane knew her tolerance had a cost. The part of her that dreamed of a deeper connection and a clear commitment from Charles was still there, quietly waiting. She often wondered if she was settling or if her ability to tolerate was a strength. She told herself that her patience would pay off, that Charles would eventually align his words with his actions, and that she could wait a little longer. But every time another month or year passed without the proposal she secretly hoped for, she couldn't help but feel a flicker of doubt. Was she waiting for something that might never happen?

The truth was that Jane's ability to tolerate was a double-edged sword. On the one hand, it allowed her to see the good in people and relationships, focusing on what worked rather than what didn't. On the other hand, it kept her stuck in situations where her needs and desires were only partially met. For so long, she conditioned herself to accept the bare minimum, believing that love was about compromise and patience, even if it meant shelving her dreams. But as much as she admired her resilience, she was beginning to question whether it was time to ask for more for herself.

Jane's journey wasn't over, and she knew that. Her tolerance, while admirable, was no longer enough. She was starting to see that wanting more didn't make her ungrateful or selfish; it made her human. And maybe, just maybe, it was time to stop tolerating and start asking for the love and commitment she truly deserved. The thought was terrifying and exhilarating, but one thing was clear: Jane was ready to rewrite the rules she had lived by for so long. And this time, she was putting herself at the center of her story.

Jane had always thought of herself as someone who could handle anything. After all, she had been navigating complicated relationships and dodging emotional landmines for most of her life. But something shifted when she started counseling. For the first time, she wasn't just brushing off her feelings or rationalizing other people's behaviors; she was diving headfirst into the root causes of her struggles. And let's be real: it was hard. Sitting in that therapist's office, peeling back the layers of her life, Jane started to see patterns she had ignored for years.

At first, she had gone to therapy to "fix" herself; after all, she figured the problems in her relationship with Charles had to be her fault. But the deeper she dug, the clearer it became that this wasn't about her being broken. It was about her finally seeing the truth, and that truth wasn't pretty. Yes, Charles sent romantic texts, made her favorite meals, and made her feel desired in ways she hadn't experienced before. However, those gestures were a Band-Aid over a deeper wound, because when Jane thought about the bigger picture, she realized something unsettling: Charles didn't treat her with the respect she deserved.

The more Jane reflected, the more obvious it became. Charles had a way of twisting conversations to make her feel like she was the problem. If she asked for something simple, like a bit of time or even help with a specific task, he would dismiss her outright or, worse, call her "needy" or "unreasonable." When she tried to bring up issues that mattered to her, he would roll his eyes, tell her she was overthinking, or accuse her of being dramatic. These moments weren't rare; they were frequent, but she had been so focused on the good that she minimized the bad.

Counseling opened Jane's eyes to a pattern she hadn't seen before. While Charles was great at the things he thought were thoughtful, he had a way of ignoring what she needed, the things she asked for. He would brush it off if she asked for support, only to later surprise her with something he thought she should appreciate. It wasn't just dismissive, it was condescending. It sent the message that her desires didn't matter as much as his vision of what the relationship should be. And when she tried to discuss how this made her feel, the gaslighting began. "You're imagining things," he'd say, or "Why are you trying to make me the bad guy?" Over time, these comments made Jane doubt herself. "Am I crazy? "Am I asking for too much?" and "Why can't I just be patient?"

Therapy helped her see these tactics for what they were: manipulation. She realized that Charles' behavior wasn't just a quirk or a misunderstanding but a pattern of control. He kept her in a cycle of gratitude and doubt, making her question her instincts while staying tethered to the version of him that occasionally seemed perfect. The counselor helped her understand that love isn't just about gestures; it's about mutual respect, listening, and making space for each other's needs. And in those areas, Charles was falling short.

Jane also began to realize how her past had shaped her tolerance for this behavior. Growing up, she learned to settle for the bare minimum, taking only what she could get and being thankful for it, even if it wasn't what she truly wanted or needed. That mindset had carried her into her relationship with Charles, and frankly, all her relationships. Where she had mistaken his small, surface-level efforts for genuine love and partnership. But now, she was learning the difference between being grateful for gestures and settling for less than she deserved. In her other relationships, it made her accept the minimal efforts of friends or family members. With statements like 'you're a good girl' or 'you helped me a lot,' she could be won over in an instant. She would remember being told nobody has to do anything for you, and you can't get mad at people for what they choose to do for you. Suck it up and keep it moving. Either you are in or out.

The revelations were not easy to swallow. Jane found herself questioning everything she thought she knew about her relationship. How much of it had been real, and how much was her clinging to an idealized version of Charles? But instead of feeling defeated, she felt empowered. She was finally seeing her situation clearly, and for the first time in years, she felt like she was regaining control over her own narrative.

Jane wasn't ready to make any big decisions yet, but she knew one thing for sure: she wasn't crazy. Her feelings, needs, and experiences were valid, and she deserved a relationship that honored them. With each session, she grew stronger, more confident, and more certain that the best version of herself was just around the corner. Jane was finally starting to see the strength and stop wondering... But am I? Whether Charles was a part of that future or not, Jane was finally learning to put herself first, and that felt like a victory in itself.

Shondra and Jane's stories highlight the same truth: trauma and loss distort how you see yourself and your worth. You start to believe the cruel voices in your head more than the kind ones outside of you. But here's the thing:

- The fight isn't about proving others wrong. It's about proving yourself right.
- You are not defined by what broke you; you are defined by how you rebuild.
- The questions you're asking: Am I really strong? Am I really enough? These aren't signs of weakness. They are invitations to discover your truth.

Here's the most important part: You can change at any moment. The moment you start asking why, the moment you start getting to the root, is the moment you begin reclaiming your power. Healing isn't about going back to who you were; it's about growing into who you are becoming.

CHAPTER 5

What Do You Think

Before we proceed, I want to make it clear: I am not diagnosing or treating anyone here. If what you're reading evokes strong emotions or makes you feel overwhelmed, please reach out for professional support.

Our thoughts are the lenses through which we interpret the world around us. After an emotional (grief, betrayal, violence) upheaval, those lenses crack and can disrupt the very essence of who you are. The person you were before the trauma feels distant, almost like a memory, and the person you see in the mirror now may feel unfamiliar or even like a stranger. This fracture in identity is one of trauma's more invisible wounds, and it can be incredibly disorienting.

One of the most complex parts of this invisible fracture (I like to call them restore points) is that you don't always immediately identify the change. In the aftermath of trauma, our mind's priority is survival. We focus on getting through the day, often pushing away or ignoring the more complex feelings. When my mom passed away (restore point), there was a difference in me that I couldn't put my finger on. All I knew was I had to be strong for everyone else. I would quote scriptures... but there was still this longing, questioning, and upset that I could not explain. Years went by before I ever truly addressed my pain and sadness.

Eventually, after the pain, we start noticing that we don't feel right, something is missing or different, and it's not always easy to put into words. We may realize that we're struggling to connect with people and that we've become numb to things that once brought us happiness. Maybe we feel emptiness, a kind of hollow ache where our heart is. These are all signs that trauma has disrupted our identities, that there's a fracture inside that needs attention and healing.

Trauma strips away a sense of safety and control, but it can also steal our sense of continuity: that feeling that we are the same person across all parts of our lives. In my book "Getting Over It," I recount a night that forever changed how I see the world and myself. **_(The next section briefly describes sexual assault. If you'd rather skip the details, jump to the next section. Please seek support if this content brings you distress.)_** It started like any other carefree evening. I had gone out with friends, ready to dance the night away, to laugh and let loose. The bass thumped through the floor, the kind that shakes you from the inside out, and I let myself be carried away by the rhythm. Drink in hand, I felt alive and free. When the night ended, I was exhausted, but it was the good kind of tiredness, the kind that comes from pure joy.

When it was time to head home, my friend said we'd all ride with her new boyfriend. The car ride was uneventful. People laughing and talking...I sat quietly, looking out the window. I hadn't told anyone that her boyfriend was someone I had known before. It didn't matter, or I told myself it didn't. I pushed the thought aside as we reached her house.

I took my shower and went to bed while they sat in the living room watching television. In the dead of the night, I felt something strange: weight, a pressure. My mind struggled to claw itself from its deep sleep, and when I finally opened my eyes, my entire world tilted. He was on top of me, and he was raping me. My body locked in place, my brain trying to catch up to the horror of what was happening. By the time I fully woke, he was done. He got up and walked out of the room without saying one word.

As he walked out of the room, he turned to look back at me, his silhouette lit by the glow of the television in the living room. That image is burned into my mind. The way his shadow seemed to mock my helplessness, the smirk on his face as if what he had done was nothing at all. I lay there, paralyzed, my heart pounding, my thoughts racing with questions. How did this happen? What just happened? How did I not wake up sooner? The questions were too much. I had to get up and get out of that house.

That night, something shattered in me (restore point). It wasn't just my sense of safety; it was my sense of self. I never slept the same way again. Every door, every window is locked, not just with a key, but with the lingering fear of what happens when you think you are safe, but you aren't.

I confronted him before I moved away, but it didn't bring me peace. I thought maybe facing him would give me back a piece of what he stole. I told him quietly, you didn't break me, but the truth is that event changed me in ways I wasn't ready to admit, not even to myself. I chose not to share with my friends or family. I told almost no one; partly to protect myself, partly because I didn't want a storm I couldn't control. I moved to another state within weeks. I called it my "fresh start." The truth was, I was running from the shattered pieces of me.

Trauma (restore point) doesn't just steal your safety. It fractures your identity. It takes the confident, vibrant version of yourself and buries her under shame, doubt, and silence.

Unstoppable: A 5 step Guide to Reclaiming Identity & Purpose

When we go through trauma, our thinking shifts. Sometimes it's subtle, and we become numb to things we once enjoyed. At other times, it is all-consuming, spiraling into questions like, 'What's wrong with me?' Why does this keep happening? Who am I now?

There's a word for this hidden war it's called cognitive dissonance. It's the mental tug of war when what we believe doesn't match how we behave, or when what we value doesn't line up with how we're living. Perhaps you take pride in being strong, but you find yourself isolating and avoiding. Maybe you value health, but you're numbing with habits that harm you. This discomfort isn't proof that you're weak; it's proof that your mind is trying to reconcile the fracture.

Let's revisit Shondra.

Shondra woke up to another day of feeling like her life was on autopilot. The same heavy thoughts, gray cloud over her head, and the nagging question How did I get here? Deep down, she knew something wasn't right. She felt out of sync with herself, like the person she was on the outside didn't match who she was on the inside. The discomfort was hard to ignore, and she couldn't help but wonder why it felt like she was constantly at war with herself.

It took a while, but Shondra finally acknowledged the discomfort instead of brushing it off. She realized that pretending everything was okay wasn't helping; It only worsened her tension. She had withdrawn from the world, isolating herself from friends, and let self-doubt rule her thoughts. Why am I acting like someone I don't even recognize? She asked herself.

Shondra knew she couldn't fix everything overnight, but she decided to make small changes to align her beliefs with her actions. She started by being kind to herself. When the voice of doubt crept in, telling her she wasn't good enough, she countered it with a different thought. I'm allowed to grow and change. She also began reaching out to friends that she had been avoiding. At first, it felt awkward, but she began to feel a little more like herself with each conversation. She also set boundaries with her time and energy, learning to say no to things that didn't serve her, and yes to things that brought her joy.

Little by little, Shondra started to feel more aligned with her true self. The gap between her beliefs and actions began to shrink, replaced by a sense of clarity & purpose. She wasn't perfect, and the journey wasn't smooth, but she was finally moving forward. Each small step brought her closer to the person she wanted to be, regardless of the expectations of others.

She was learning to be authentic. Being real and honest with yourself is the only way you can see change and grow. This journey is not about being perfect or having it all figured out. It's about listening to the discomfort and making small changes. Give yourself the same grace you extend to others. Now, Shondra isn't just surviving; she is rebuilding. As she looked ahead, she felt something she hadn't felt in a long time. Hope!

Part of changing your thinking is understanding how you think. Each of us processes challenges through a natural thinking style:

- Analytical- breaks things down
- Creative- imagines possibilities
- Practical- Focuses on Solutions
- Intuitive- trusts gut instincts
- Reflective- Looks inward for meaning

Most of us have multiple thinking types depending on the situation. Trauma convinces us we only have one tool, and it's broken. The truth is, we have many tools. And learning how to use them can rebuild the bridge between who we were and who we are becoming.

Have you had exaggerated or irrational thought processes? If so, it may be that you are experiencing cognitive distortion. This happens when we filter, overgeneralize, discount the positives, jump to conclusions, catastrophize, and personalize. Have you ever said:

"I always mess up?" That's an example of an overgeneralization.

"Nothing ever works out for me?" That's an example of filtering only the negative.

"If I fail, I'm worthless." That's an example of all-or-nothing thinking.

"They didn't text me back; they must hate me." = jumping to conclusions. These are distortions, and although they feel automatic, you can interrupt them, change them. You do this by catching the thought and labeling the distortion as soon as you become aware of it. You can also challenge the thought by asking if it is true. Where is the evidence? You can reframe the thought by replacing it with a balanced thought. You also want to be patient with yourself. Change isn't instant, but small changes add up.

Recognizing and addressing these distortions is essential because, if left unchecked, they repeat and can create a self-fulfilling cycle. Those negative thoughts only fuel negative emotions and behaviors. It is like a faulty code that doesn't stop but has to be completely overwritten. By learning to identify these distortions and practicing a more balanced way of thinking we can improve our emotional resilience, self-compassion, and gain a clearer, more realistic perspective of the situation. Confronting these distortions does not eliminate negative thoughts completely, but it gives you the tools to challenge and reshape them in healthier ways.

Let's look at Erica.

Erica prided herself on being the strong one, able to handle anything. She was a career woman and a dependable friend. She had built her life around being the one everyone could count on, but she felt like she was running on fumes. She poured herself into her job, into helping others, into checking every box on life's endless To Do List… but where did that leave her?

Therapy showed her a painful truth: she had been living for

everyone else. Saying yes when she meant no. Smiling when she wanted to scream.

As she sat in her car, staring blankly at the dashboard, an uneasy feeling settled in her chest, a feeling she had been ignoring for far too long. Something wasn't right. She wasn't just tired; She was resentful.

She thought back to all the times she had brushed off that nagging feeling. The times she had sacrificed her peace for the sake of keeping the peace. Why did I let this happen? Her thoughts raced, and her mind became flooded with memories, and the answer was swift: saying no wasn't comfortable, felt selfish, and she wanted people to like her. She had spent so many years defining herself by what she did for others that she didn't know who she was outside of that. However, none of these were the reasons, although they were all true statements; the truth was she no longer felt like the strong confident person she used to be. . As a result, she required external validation. After the trauma, she began to define herself by what others thought was acceptable and beautiful.

That day, Erica set one small boundary. She said no. She called a friend for support, and she promised herself that she would stop living out of obligation and start living her life with intention.

As she pulled out of the parking lot, a quiet sense of relief settled over her. She didn't have it all figured out yet, but for the first time in a long time, she wasn't running from the truth; she was facing it head-on.

As she started releasing things, she made room for the things that felt genuinely exciting and fulfilling in the present. Instead of asking herself what she should be doing, she asked herself what she wanted to do, what made her excited, or what new thing she wanted to learn. She wasn't quite sure who this new version would be, but she knew she wanted her to be someone who lived with intention and found meaning in small, authentic moments. She began to do things she hadn't given herself permission to do before.

Embracing the flexibility to change allowed her to be kinder to herself. She focused on building a resilient and real identity that could grow with her as she continued to heal. She learned to trust herself in a way she had never done before, to listen to what felt true, and let that guide her. Building a new identity can be messy and complicated, but it's also one of the most empowering things you can ever do.

The truth is you're not broken. Trauma may have caused some fractures, but fractures can heal. You don't have to become who you were before. That version of you did her job; she got you here. Now it's time for the stronger, wiser, and more authentic version to emerge because the cracks don't define you. They become places of awareness, and that's where healing begins.

CHAPTER 6

LET IT GO

Listen to me and hear me well. You are not who you used to be. They are not who they used to be. Things change, and people change, and holding on to the past will keep you stuck. The truth is, at some point, you have to decide to LET IT GO.

That sounds amazing, right? But how many times have you tried to let something go, and just couldn't? It stuck in your mind, being replayed for years. That old betrayal, that failed relationship, that lost dream, even a former glory. It clings to you like a shadow. In this chapter, we're going to talk about releasing the identities, beliefs, and roles that no longer serve you so you can step into a more authentic you.

There are parts of your life that feel familiar and comfortable, like your favorite shirt from twenty or thirty years ago that might be a little to snug. Perhaps you're still holding onto old titles or roles, such as 'peacemaker' or 'good girl.' At one point, those roles had purpose, but now they feel draining. Growth will require shedding. When we hold on too tightly to outdated titles, habits, or relationships, we create inner conflict. A career that once felt like a calling may now feel like a cage. A relationship that once nurtured you may now feel toxic. A belief that once protected you may now be keeping you small.

Letting go isn't about rejecting your past; it's about honoring your journey.

When you release those parts of the old you, it can feel like grief. But this process requires honesty, courage, and a willingness to look inward with clear eyes. Do you still hold the same values or beliefs that align with the title that you value so much? We change and evolve, and as we do, we don't have to feel bad about the choices and decisions we make that align with who we are now or who we are becoming.

You might mourn an identity you've outgrown: caregiver, hustler, overachiever. You might feel sadness when walking away from relationships that no longer serve you. That grief is real and valid. But loss creates space. Think of it like cleaning a garden: pulling weeds so new flowers can bloom. By letting go of what doesn't fit, you make room for peace, joy, and alignment with your authentic self.

Knowing when to let go, even in personal relationships, is a crucial life skill that can lead to greater emotional well-being and personal growth. Often, we cling to relationships, situations, or beliefs that no longer serve us out of fear, habit, or a misplaced sense of loyalty. However, recognizing when it's time to release these attachments can be both liberating and eye-opening, and open the door to new opportunities and healthier connections.

We think everyone we befriend is meant to be there for life, but sometimes relationships are meant to be temporary. We may want to hold on to these relationships, but some people are not meant to be in our lives forever. I believe some people are assignments, and they may have been placed in your life to teach or be taught by you. If you experience constant conflicts, lack of mutual respect, or a persistent feeling of emotional drain, these may be clear red flags of a relationship in trouble. If you find yourself consistently compromising your values, suppressing your true self, or feeling lonely when you're together, it may be time to reassess the relationship. If trust has been irreparably broken or if your goals and values have diverged significantly... over time, holding on to the relationship may be doing more harm than good.

However, letting go doesn't always mean ending a relationship entirely. Sometimes, it means releasing unrealistic expectations, outdated roles, or unhealthy patterns within the relationship. This process requires honest communication, self-reflection, and often, a willingness to seek outside help through counseling or therapy. Remember, letting go is not about giving up but about making space for growth, healing, and potentially more fulfilling connections. It's a courageous act of self-care that acknowledges that change is a natural part of life and that sometimes the healthiest thing we can do is release what no longer fits.

Remember that letting go of parts of your old identity can feel like a genuine loss. You might experience sadness, anxiety, or a sense of disorientation as you release familiar aspects of your identity. This is normal and necessary. Allow yourself space to breathe. If you're letting go of the role of caregiver after years of looking after a loved one, it's natural to feel a mix of relief and loss. If you're shedding the identity of workaholic to prioritize your health and relationships, you might mourn the sense of purpose or validation that role once provided.

Let's go back to our story about Jessica.

Jessica knew she couldn't stay in that dark place forever. The grief was still there; it wasn't something she could pack away, but she began to realize that staying stuck in anger and despair would not honor her mother's memory. Lisa was a woman of unwavering strength and a beacon of hope for everyone she encountered. Jessica couldn't let her pain steal that legacy.

Slowly, and with a lot of hesitation, she began to explore what it might look like to change her thinking after losing her mom.

At first, it felt impossible. Every time she tried to change her thoughts, the grief and pain pulled her back. She felt overwhelmed, asking herself How can I move forward when I feel so broken? Why should I feel happy when I feel so much sadness and pain? But then she remembered something her mother used to say, paraphrasing Dr Martin Luther King Jr.: Sometimes the only way through is step by step. You don't have to see the whole path, just your next step... that became her mantra. Jessica realized she didn't have to have all the answers, and she didn't have to heal overnight. She just had to take the next step, no matter how small.

Jessica started a gratitude journal, writing down even the smallest things that made her grateful. She learned to let herself feel her emotions instead of trying to talk herself out of them. In the past, she had always been told she shouldn't be angry, but now she would ask herself, why did I get angry or What can I learn from this? Do I need to create a new boundary? How can I grow? You don't have to be defined by moments of emotion. Her grief had taught her how to be resilient, her anger taught her how to create boundaries, and her loss taught her how to value every moment.

One of the most significant breakthroughs came when Jessica decided to reconnect with her faith. At first, it felt awkward, even hypocritical, to turn back to God after all the time she had spent blaming Him, but she knew that deep down, her mother's faith, her own faith, had been their anchor. She started small, reading a verse here and saying a short prayer there. Over time, those moments became less about obligation and more about relationship. Her faith didn't look the same as it had before, but it started to feel like a source of strength instead of a source of pain.

Jessica began to rebuild her life, realizing she didn't have to ignore her grief or pretend everything was fine. Instead it was about choosing hope, about being intentional even when it felt out of reach. It was about honoring her mother's legacy, not by staying stuck in sorrow but by living the kind of life Lisa would have wanted for her: a life filled with purpose, love, and growth.

Letting go also requires self-awareness. There are two key types of self-awareness: Internal and External. Internal Self-awareness is about understanding your feelings, values, and your interests. It's about being in tune with yourself, understanding what motivates you, and how you respond to the world around you. Sometimes, where we get it wrong is external self-awareness, which is understanding how others perceive you. It's about recognizing how your actions will affect those around you and how you fit into the bigger picture. Both forms of self-awareness will create a balance between how you connect with others.

Being self-aware boosts your emotional intelligence. It can enhance leadership by making you more authentic. It helps you respect yourself more and gives you greater control over your reactions by enabling you to identify your triggers. Self-awareness equips you to live life with clarity, and it doesn't happen overnight. Start by practicing mindfulness, sit still and listen, pay attention to your thoughts and emotions. Ask your friends how they perceive you. Even meditation can deepen your connection with your inner self, sharpening your emotions and feelings, and allow you to hear what your body and surroundings are saying to you.

Of course, there are challenges along the way. Cognitive biases will distort how you see yourself. Emotional barriers, such as fear and insecurity, can cloud your ability to be honest. Finding time to meditate can be a challenge, especially in today's world of constant distractions, where even focusing can seem like a daunting task. The rewards of increased self-awareness are life-changing.

Self-awareness is an ongoing journey, and as you grow and change, your awareness will also change. Doing regular check-ins, being open to feedback, and being open to honest criticism are essential for maintaining and deepening this awareness. The beauty of self-awareness is that it empowers you to be more intentional and navigate every challenge you face with a clear mind. It will enable you to embrace growth and change and connect with the world in a way that feels authentic to you. It's not just a skill but a lifelong gift.

As you become more aware of yourself and your thoughts, you will see how they have impacted your belief system. You will be able to determine how it has affected your relationships, self-worth, career, health, body image, and even your thoughts about money.

One way to support your emotional health and well-being is to practice reflection. Reflection allows you to notice negative thoughts as they occur. It's also valuable to seek feedback from trusted friends, family members, or therapists. Sometimes others can see patterns in our behavior or thinking that we can't see. They may notice recurring patterns in your conversations, such as how everyone treats you in a certain way. It's time to stop and reflect on determining whether this external perspective can provide invaluable insight into the beliefs we need to release.

Your beliefs shape your reality. Your beliefs are how you interpret data; therefore, if you believe all people are evil, when you interact with people, you will already have:

1. A preconceived notion

2. Fears or doubts based on your beliefs

3. Deeply rooted validated beliefs

These make it harder to let it go. This will be your reality until you allow yourself to open your heart to vulnerability and new experiences.

Our beliefs are powerful; they shape a significant portion of who we are, how we think, and even how we perceive ourselves and our abilities. Your belief is the foundation of your thoughts, emotions, and actions. Some are conscious and easy to recognize, and some lie beneath the surface, subtly guiding our decisions and behavior. They can be empowering or limiting.

To let go of those limiting beliefs, you must 1. Identify them. 2. Take time for self-reflection 3. Question your assumptions, 4. Observe your emotional reactions, 5. Observe absolutes like always or never. Seek feedback from others and 6. Explore and reflect on your past. 7. Give yourself grace. Once you identify these limiting beliefs, it's important to approach the process of releasing them and letting them go with compassion and patience.

Remember that these beliefs often develop as coping mechanisms and defense strategies to protect yourself. This mindset will set the stage for the next steps in your journey: challenging and replacing limiting beliefs with more empowering alternatives.

Let's look at Sarah from an earlier story.

Sarah used to think of herself as the queen of keeping the peace. She would smile when she wanted to scream, nod when she wanted to say no, and bite her tongue when she had every reason to speak up. On the outside, she seemed like the perfect friend, the ideal coworker, the one everyone could count on. But inside, Sarah was a mess. She wasn't keeping the peace; she was bottling up frustration, resentment, and a deep sense of not being good enough. And to top it all off, she had developed a severe case of Irritable Bowel Syndrome (IBS), which felt like her body's way of yelling Hey, stop pretending everything's fine!

For years, Sarah's life was dominated by one big, limiting belief: 'If I'm not needed, I'm not valuable.' That belief turned her into the ultimate people pleaser. She said yes to everything, took on everyone's problems, and went out of her way to avoid upsetting anyone. But the more she tried to make others happy, the more passive-aggressive she became. She would agree to plans she didn't want to make, then quietly sulk while she was there. She would take on extra work, but secretly resented that her coworkers were not helping. It was an exhausting cycle.

Then came the moment that changed everything. After an excruciating bout with her IBS, Sarah's doctor sat her down and said Stress is killing you. If you don't make some changes, you will only get worse. That was the wake-up call she needed. Sarah immediately realized she could not keep living this way, not just for her health but for her happiness. So, she decided it was time to let go of the beliefs that had been holding her back.

The first step was tough. Sarah had to face the truth that her need to be needed wasn't as noble as she thought it was, but it was fear in disguise. Fear of being unimportant. Fear of being rejected. Fear of not being enough. She had to challenge that voice in her head that said, "If you say no, they'll stop caring about you." And while it wasn't easy, she felt freer each time she set a boundary or said what was on her mind.

Sarah also began focusing on herself for the first time in years. She started journaling, asking herself what she wanted instead of what everyone else expected. She rediscovered her love of painting, a passion she hadn't pursued since college. She took long walks without her phone, soaking in the quiet and learning to enjoy her own company. As she let go of the need to be needed, she realized something amazing: the people who cared about her didn't need her to be everything to them. They just needed her to be herself.

And then, as if by magic, her IBS started to heal. No more waking up in pain or skipping meals because of the discomfort. Sarah felt like a weight had been lifted, both physically and emotionally. For the first time in forever, she wasn't carrying the burden of everyone else's expectations. Sarah's life wasn't perfect, but it was hers. She still had moments of doubt, but now she knew how to pause, breathe, and remind herself that she was enough just as she was. Letting go of her limiting beliefs didn't just change her; it set her free. And as she moved forward, one thing was clear: the best version of Sarah was the one who lived for herself, not for anyone else.

Identifying beliefs to release is a powerful act of self-awareness and the first step toward powerful transformation. By recognizing the beliefs that hold you back, you open the door to new possibilities and growth. I learned to use some of these techniques in my own life, and they have helped me tremendously. Anytime I use the words *"Always"* or *"Never,"* I know I am exaggerating. It immediately calms my body, and I return to a state of rational thinking.

Remember, this is an ongoing process and letting go isn't a weakness. It isn't giving up, it's strength, it's clarity. It's choosing peace and alignment. You don't have to erase your past and deny the lessons. But you do have to decide: Will my past define me or refine me? This is where divine timing comes in, knowing that you are where you are supposed to be at the right time. Free yourself to stop living by deadlines and ticking clocks.

When you cling to what's over, you are trying to force things to be what they aren't; you're living in fear of time, thinking you are missing out on something. When you release the expectation of doing things by a specific time and living by what has happened in the past, you make room for those divine moments and breakthroughs that occur at just the right moment.

When you let go of something, you are making room for the person or thing that is meant to fill it. The key is trust:

- Trust yourself
- Trust the process
- Trust the journey

Letting go without it feels like you're falling, but letting go with trust feels like flying.

I invite you to stop trying to control every outcome, stop replaying old stories, and stop saying you missed your moment. You didn't, you are exactly where you're supposed to be, right here, right now. When you finally surrender control, you realize what you thought you lost was only clearing a path for what was meant for you all along.

The freedom you're searching for is waiting on the other side of release.

So take a breath, unclench your fists, and let it go.

CHAPTER 7

DON'T HOLD YOUR BREATH

We've all heard the saying at some point in our lives, "Don't hold your breath!" Usually, it's a warning not to expect much, not to get your hopes up. But what if you actually tried? What happens when you hold your breath waiting for something to happen? You suffocate. You weaken. You stay still.

Sometimes we hold our breath in fear, hoping the storm will pass—other times in anticipation, waiting for the "perfect" moment to arrive. Either way, holding your breath doesn't protect you; it traps you. It locks you in a cycle of inaction, leaving you powerless and anxious.

Trauma can do the same thing. It leaves us suspended in fear or anticipation, holding our breath while life passes us by. We wait for the apology that never comes. The phone call that never comes in. The perfect moment that never arrives. And just like holding your breath, it isn't sustainable. You're not meant to live frozen, in suspended animation. You're meant to inhale, exhale, and move forward, step by step.

Holding your breath isn't always obvious. It may look like procrastination, stalling that important conversation, avoiding a decision, or endlessly waiting for the "right time." Sometimes it shows you as being busy, doing everything except the one thing that matters most.

Ask yourself: Am I stuck because I don't know what to do or because I'm afraid of doing it? That one question reveals the difference between confusion and fear. And fear, when left unchecked, keeps you paralyzed.

When you avoid action, anxiety grows. Consider the last time you delayed making a decision. Was it relief you felt? Or was it more "what-ifs" piling on top of each other? Procrastination is like holding your breath: Your heart races, your body tenses, your mind loops. Yet nothing changes. And here's the truth, clarity doesn't come while you're frozen. It comes when you take that first step, even if it's small or uncertain.

Remember Sarah?

Sarah always wanted someone to validate her pain and her feelings. She waited in anticipation for approval. Whenever someone mistreated her, cut her off in conversation, overlooked her effort, or dismissed her feelings, she would swallow her words and wait. Wait for them to notice. Wait for them to apologize. Wait for them to validate her pain.

The apologies rarely came. Instead, Sarah found herself replaying scenarios in her head, holding her breath, hoping that maybe tomorrow someone would finally see her, value her, and treat her the way she longed to be treated. The longer she held her breath for that moment of validation, the heavier the silence became, the more resentful she became.

Deep down, Sarah's need for approval wasn't about the people around her; it was about the belief she carried inside: My opinion only matters when others agree with it or when people approve of me. That belief bound her to a cycle of anticipation and disappointment. Every time she waited for someone else to give her permission to feel, she gave away her power. On the outside, she looked agreeable, but on the inside, she was drowning.

Sarah was emotionally holding her breath.

One day, after another long night of replaying a disagreement in her head, Sarah had an epiphany: What if I stop waiting for others to give me permission? In that moment, Sarah realized what many of us miss: when life shakes us, it's tempting to hold our breath and wait for clarity. Those disagreements or disappointments throw you for a loop and challenge everything you thought you knew about yourself. It's easy to freeze up, but here's the truth: holding your breath during those chaotic moments only keeps you stuck, weighing you down with anxiety, making it harder for you to see the exciting possibilities that are right in front of you.

She realized that waiting for others to validate her feelings and her pain was killing her and her spirit. She realized that if she wanted release, she had to breathe for herself by speaking her truth, setting boundaries, and stopping waiting for permission to matter.

So, we must follow the steps and the process. First, you have to recognize when you are holding your breath to break free from the cycle. It doesn't always look like full-blown paralysis. Sometimes, it's subtle, such as delaying an important conversation, avoiding decisions, or constantly waiting for the "right" opportunity. It may feel like procrastination or even busyness with unimportant tasks, allowing us to prevent tackling what truly matters. But at its core, holding your breath is a fear response, keeping you in a state of procrastination. Ask yourself: Am I stuck because I don't know what to do, or because I'm afraid of doing this? That single question can reveal a lot.

We talked about procrastination putting you in a holding pattern, like holding your breath. Procrastination can take a significant toll on you. Your mind races with "what-ifs" while the fear grows bigger the longer you stay in the state of procrastination. Holding your breath, both literally and figuratively, puts your body and mind into a stress cycle. Your heart races, your muscles tense, and you're stuck in anticipation mode, waiting for something to happen. It's exhausting, right? Your body is constantly fighting itself.

But here's the big secret: Holding your breath doesn't solve anything. It's a survival mechanism, triggered by fear, and it doesn't protect you from the outcome that you're afraid of. In fact, it can make things more complicated. Fear often clouds your judgment, keeping you from seeing the opportunities and solutions that are right in front of you. The truth is that clarity and confidence don't magically appear while you Procrastinate. It comes when you start moving, even if the first step feels small and uncertain.

So, what's causing this fear? Fear is a sign that something matters to you. If you weren't scared, it might mean you didn't care. Instead of seeing fear as a stop sign, try to reframe it as a guide. What is fear trying to tell you in that situation? Maybe it's pointing to something you value or sincerely want but are afraid to reach for. Recognizing this can turn fear from a roadblock into a motivator.

What about anticipation? We wait, hoping for the perfect moment to reveal itself and all the pieces to align before we act. But life doesn't work that way. The truth is that the "perfect moment" is a myth. The "perfect moment" is that magical, idealized point in time we often imagine where everything aligns flawlessly. The truth is that the perfect moment is a trap because it feels safe to stay still. But it is just fear in disguise. Waiting only robs you of growth, while action (even small steps) creates momentum.

During these moments of waiting, we tell ourselves things like: "I'll start when I'm more prepared," or "I'll do it when I have more money, more time, or more support." But the truth is, no amount of waiting will make us feel completely ready because growth requires moving even when you're uncomfortable or unsure.

What draws us into these perfect moments is that it feels safe, it allows us to wait. However, by waiting, we shield ourselves from potential failure, rejection, or mistakes. But the irony is that waiting costs us more than the risk of failure or rejection. It keeps us stuck in a cycle of inaction, robbing us of opportunities to learn, grow, and achieve the things that we genuinely want.

Here's the real secret code: the perfect moment isn't something you wait for; it's something you create. It happens when you decide to act despite fear, uncertainty, or any imperfection. It's about starting where you are with what you have, trusting that with each step you take, the next step will become clearer. It's not about having all the answers; it's about having the courage to take that step. So, let go of the idea that everything must be "just right" before you start. Embrace the messiness, the small beginnings, the imperfections, and the failures you make along the way, because in those moments, you're perfecting the process... and oftentimes, we end up creating someone else's perfect moments.

Letting go of the fear and anticipation starts with one simple act: exhaling. It's about releasing tension and making space for action, no matter how small. When you let go of the idea that everything must be perfect, you begin to see power in YOUR steps. Each move forward is a decision to stop allowing fear to take control and to start creating the life you want. It's not about fixing everything all at once; it's about shifting your focus from waiting to doing.

As I write this, I'm reminded of the classic movie *Waiting to Exhale.* The film centers on four women navigating love, life, and heartbreak, each in their own way. Throughout the movie, they're all figuratively holding their breath, waiting for things and patterns to unfold, waiting for love to feel real, waiting for validation from others, waiting for something outside of them to fix their lives. Sound familiar yet? The title itself is a metaphor for that moment of release when they finally let go of the things that hold them back and begin to reclaim control of their lives. To me, their journey mirrors what I'm talking about here, moving from fear and anticipation to empowerment, freedom, and action.

The beauty of starting small is that it's doable. Just like the women in the movie, you don't have to solve everything at once. Think about Savannah (Whitney Houston's character); she struggled with being stuck in an unhealthy relationship because she thought it might lead to happiness. Her eventual decision to walk away was her exhaling, a small but powerful act of reclaiming her self-worth.

That same approach works when you're moving past fear. Instead of staring at the entire mountain, focus on the next step in front of you. Whether it's having a conversation you've been avoiding, writing down a goal, or saying yes to a new opportunity. Each small action builds momentum. And momentum is everything when it comes to getting unstuck.

When your confidence grows, it becomes easier to take bigger, bolder steps. Suddenly, the fear that once had you paralyzed begins to lose its grip.

So now that you've taken action, let's celebrate those wins, no matter how small, because they're a BIG DEAL! They are proof that you're moving and choosing courage over comfort. Think about Gloria (Loretta Devine's character); she opened herself up to love again after years of putting herself last. It didn't happen overnight. She constantly put her child and her ex-husband first, but one day she took a step that allowed her to live a life that felt full and authentic. She realized that she deserved to be happy and not allow herself to be a doormat or a convenience for everyone else. Just like in the movie, celebrate progress; it will fuel your desire to keep moving forward. Remember, don't look back, don't look back. ☺

Remember progress isn't a straight line, it zigzags, stumbles, and course corrects... but motion is motion.

As you allow yourself to discover this newfound confidence and begin to build momentum, you will realize the immense power you possess. Fear may come and whisper to you in the background, but it will no longer control your emotions and decisions. You will begin to make choices that align with your goals and values. You will start to have a sense of control that feels transformative; it will change how you see yourself and what you believe you're capable of. And the best part is that you don't have to do it alone. Just like the women in Waiting to Exhale, who supported each other and found strength in their friendships, you can also be strategic in the friendships and alliances you build as you reframe your new narrative for your life. When you create this support system, it becomes easier to keep or build your momentum and stay consistent.

As you build your support system, it is essential to remember that your power comes from within. Nobody can take the steps for you, but they can walk next to you. Leaning on others is not a sign of weakness; it's a sign of strength. It shows that you are willing to do what it takes to grow and thrive. When you combine your internal drive with external support, you become *UNSTOPPABLE.*

So, take a deep breath literally and figuratively. Let go of the fear that's been holding you back and take the first step forward. It may not feel earth-shattering right now, but with each step forward, everything changes. Just like the women in Waiting to Exhale, your journey towards confidence and empowerment doesn't require perfection; it requires persistence. Stop holding your breath. It's time to exhale and move forward.

Exhaling means letting go of fear, perfection, and waiting for validation. It means taking action even when your knees shake. Like the women in *Waiting to Exhale,* your breakthrough comes when you stop holding your breath for someone else's approval, apology, or permission and start breathing for yourself.

Exhale because holding your breath keeps you in bondage

Exhale, because waiting robs you of your future.

Exhale, because you are unstoppable when you decide to move.

CHAPTER 8

Vision: It's a Whole new World

Your entire life can change in a single moment. Not because your circumstances shift, but because you do. I remember the first time I heard the term' paradigm shift'... let me tell you, I was hooked on the concept. The idea that you could change the entire trajectory of your thoughts and life just by rewiring the framework (approach or belief) behind them.... Mind... Blown. It felt both incredibly simple and deeply complex at the same time, like someone had handed me the keys to my own mind.

 Here's the thing: A paradigm is more than a mindset. It's a deep-rooted belief that quietly shapes everything: what you believe is possible, how you interpret the world, and even how you see yourself. And here's the truth: Your perception, the way you interpret any situation in the moment, will never rise higher than your paradigm.

Think about it this way: your perception is the lens you're looking through, but your paradigm is the prescription in that lens. You can clean the glass, adjust the angle, and look for the silver lining, but if the prescription itself is wrong, the view will always be distorted. That's why real transformation doesn't start with seeing things differently in the moment; it begins with changing the system that decides what you see in the first place.

So, what does this mean in simple terms? Have you ever noticed that if you buy a red Volvo suddenly, on the highway, every vehicle you see is either red or a Volvo, or both? You buy one, and suddenly it feels like they are everywhere. Did the number of red Volvos on the road suddenly explode overnight? No, but your mind, wired by a new belief (I own a red Volvo), is now tuned to find them. Your focus always follows what you believe is true.

Proverbs 23:7 says, "As a man thinketh in his heart, so is he." This isn't about fleeting thoughts; it's about the heart and mind connection that cements your paradigm. What your heart trusts, your mind justifies, and your actions carry out. If your heart believes you're unworthy, you will filter everything through that lens, no matter how positive you try to think. However, if your heart and mind align around a new truth, your perception naturally and permanently changes.

Here's where most of us get stuck: we try to change how we see things (mind) without changing the underlying belief. We force ourselves to think thoughts that are contrary, for example, I may force myself to "think happy thoughts" or "stay positive" to get through the moment. That does nothing; you have to change what you believe. That's why you had the negative thought in the first place. Your old framework will continue to pull you back into the same loops of fear, doubt, and overthinking. It's like rearranging furniture in a house whose foundation is cracked. The room may look different for a while, but eventually the same problems will resurface.

When I finally understood this, I realized that the most powerful question I could ask myself wasn't, "How can I see this differently?" but "What belief is making me see it this way?" That's the difference between polishing the lens and changing the prescription. One gives you temporary clarity. The other changes your view of life.

I like to think of paradigms like the clothes hanging in your mental closet. Some still fit perfectly and make you feel amazing, others are outdated, too tight, or just ugly. But because you've had them for so long, you don't even question whether or not they feel right or wrong; they still belong because they're a part of how and what you believe.

I recommend that you complete a self-audit; it's your chance to sort through your mental closet. Ask yourself:

- What beliefs do I have about myself that feel heavy or limiting?
- Where do I feel stuck?
- Are these beliefs really mine, or did I inherit them from family, culture, or past pain?

You may find that you have beliefs that you didn't even know you're carrying. And here's the truth: until you confront them, they'll keep shaping your perception, your choices, and your outcomes. As you complete your self-audit, you'll discover things you believe in, and you will notice patterns in the people around you. This is where it gets tricky: sometimes our beliefs keeps us holding onto relationships or situations long after the evidence says we should let go.

Let's say you uncover a repeated pattern, a person who lies to you repeatedly. You catch it, you feel hurt, but you still choose to **believe** in their words. Why? Because your belief says, "people can change if I love them enough," or "I'd rather hold on to this relationship than to be alone." The problem is that your belief is colliding with the conflict or pain you feel (heart). And no matter how much you shift your thinking, if you ignore the reality of their behavior (how it makes you feel), you'll keep getting the same outcome.

Patterns reveal truth. Paradigms shape whether or not you accept that truth.

Shifting your belief in this area might look like replacing *"Love means giving a person endless chances"* with *"Love also means setting boundaries."* Or instead of thinking, "If *I let go, I will be alone,"* with *"If I let go, I make space for what's healthy."* Your new paradigm has to match your reality, not wishful thinking, if you want your perception to be accurate and your choices to make you feel free.

Let's meet Lynn. Lynn always saw herself as a play-it-safe type of person. Her identity was rooted in stability and caution. This was reinforced by her family's emphasis on financial security above all else. She followed the script: a steady job, a predictable schedule, and careful with money. Then, one morning, she walked into work and was told her position was being eliminated. Just like that, her safety net was gone. She initially began to panic. Her old paradigm began to kick in. Find another safe job, any job. As she began to complete applications, she had a nagging thought that continued to resurface: Is this really what I want, or what I believe I should want? She realized she had been treating job security like a life raft when it really had been an anchor.

Lynn began to ask herself different questions, and instead of taking the first "safe" offer, she invested in training for a business idea she had been quietly dreaming about for years. It wasn't easy, and there were months she questioned everything, but within two years, she had built a thriving business doing work she loved. Her new paradigm? Flexibility creates opportunity, and safety doesn't always mean stability.

We also have Mike. Mike's story shows the same principle. Mike is a classic example of someone who struggled with imposter syndrome in his career. Mike had always been a perfectionist, convinced he wasn't "naturally talented" enough and thought he was one step away from people realizing he was an imposter.

He was known for his work ethic and meticulous attention to detail, and yet he never believed he was good enough. No matter how much praise he got, the voice of perfectionism drowned it out.

When he was in meetings, he would prepare for hours but still hesitate to speak up, convinced he didn't have anything valuable to add. Projects took twice as long because he obsessed over every tiny detail. On the outside, he looked like a high performer; on the inside, he was exhausted.

One day, a mentor told him, "Perfectionism isn't excellence, it's fear dressed up in nice clothes." That hit him hard. Mike began to see how his old belief system and thoughts of "I'm never enough" were shaping every choice he made. Mike realized that his perfectionism and self-doubt were holding him back more than any real limitation ever could. Mike decided to try a new paradigm: "Doing something matters more than being perfect."

At first, it felt awkward. He spoke up in meetings without ever preparing. He turned in projects when they were solid instead of flawless. And nothing terrible happened; in fact, people began to notice his confidence in leadership. Little by little, the old belief began to lose its grip. His new paradigm gave him permission to take risks, trust his skills, and finally enjoy the work he had been doing all along.

Different stories, same truth: when you change your belief, your heart agrees, and your actions follow. This is the heart & mind connection that seals any deal.

When your paradigm shifts, life doesn't just look different, it feels different. Not because every circumstance magically improves, but because you're operating from a new way of thinking that changes what you notice, how you respond, and what you believe is possible. Fear of the unknown starts to loosen its grip. Instead of clinging to uncertainty, you begin to see uncertainty as a possibility. That's because your new belief tells you the unknown isn't something to fear; it's where growth lives.

As you begin to shift how you see things, curiosity becomes a powerful asset. Old belief systems ask, "What if it all falls apart?" New belief systems ask, "What's the best thing that could happen?" That single shift in energy moves you from hesitation to exploration. Suddenly, failure becomes feedback, setbacks become lessons, and challenges are invitations to grow.

Curiosity also gives you permission to take action without knowing the full outcome. Life rarely hands out guarantees, but when you stop demanding certainty before you move, you open yourself up to opportunities you couldn't have planned for. This is where some of the most meaningful shifts happen in the space between the leap and the landing.

When you shift your belief system, you also rewire the way you see your own personal power. In a fixed, fear-based belief system, it's easy to live in victim mode, blaming circumstances, other people, or bad luck for your situation. In an empowered belief system, you still acknowledge what you can't control, but you refuse to give it the final say. Instead of asking, "Why is this happening to me?" You start asking, "What can I do about this?" That one question pulls you out of helplessness and into problem solving mode. A simple way to build this habit is to make a list of what's within your control right now, even if it's small, and focus your energy there instead of dwelling on what is outside your control.

Belief system shifts rarely occur in a single lightning-bolt moment. Often, they're built through small, intentional choices made over and over. Each time you question an old belief, replace it with a new one, and act on it. When you do this, you're reinforcing your new beliefs. The more you live in your new belief system, the more natural it becomes. Eventually, you won't have to force yourself to see opportunities instead of obstacles; it will become automatic.

To live beyond your limits, you must refuse to ignore patterns in yourself and others that contradict your belief system. You have to practice your new beliefs until they become the lens through which you see without effort. Pick one belief that's been holding you back. Write it down. Then write the belief you want to replace it with. This isn't about wishful thinking; it's about building a Way of doing things that match the life you want to create. Every time you choose that new belief over the old ones, you're not shifting how you see things in the moment; you are rewriting the mental system that decides what you see. And that's when you truly begin to see beyond the limits.

Chapter Nine

Beast Mode: Hitting back

The first time I heard the phrase *Beast mode*, it hit me like a punch to the gut. Dr. Eric Thomas a.k.a. ET The Hip Hop Preacher wasn't just talking, he was commanding. His words were raw, apologetic, and precisely what I needed to hear. He made it clear: there's no room for excuses when you're in beast mode. It's about focus, grit, and putting in the work no matter how hard it gets. When I hear the words Beast Mode now, something flips inside me. It's a signal: it's time to stop whining, stop waiting, and start grinding. No matter what's in front of me, I know I have the strength to fight through it because giving up is not an option.

Here's Olivia; she knew this battle all too well. She had just received another rejection e-mail on her phone, saying, "We've decided to go in a different direction. "Another thank you for applying, but... she swallowed hard, trying to fight the lump rising in her throat. Ten Years. Ten years in education. Ten years of pouring everything she had into her students, going above and beyond, staying late, and mentoring young teachers. She had done the work. She had earned this. So why, after all these years, was she still stuck in the same position while others, some with less experience, kept moving up?

The answer came to her quickly, like a whisper cutting through her frustration. Because you don't believe you belong at the top.

The thought stung because she knew it was true. She had been playing small, accepting whatever was handed to her, convincing herself that if she just kept working hard, one day the right people would notice her. But deep down, she never believed she was worthy of more.

Not anymore.

Olivia took a deep breath, and she stared at her reflection in the rearview mirror. She remembered the phrase Beast Mode. She felt it ignite a fire in her gut, an energy she hadn't tapped into before. She wasn't going to wait anymore; she wasn't going to let self-doubt rob her of her success. It was time to stop playing by invisible rules that didn't serve her.

That's the essence of Beast Mode. It's not about being fearless. It's about acting in spite of fear. It's about pulling fuel from your frustration instead of letting it consume you. It's the moment you stop rehearsing your excuses and start proving to yourself what's already true: that you're stronger than this. Here is the truth: the version of you that went through the trauma, the rejection, the identity crisis that person doesn't define you anymore. They toughened you. And now it's time to hit back.

That night, Olivia sat down with her notebook and wrote down all her educational accomplishments, including initiatives she had led. Then she wrote the truth: I am worthy and capable of leadership. She repeated this to herself until she felt that heart-mind connection. Until she believed it in her heart and soul. Until her paradigm shifted.

Olivia went all in. She revamped her resume, tailoring it to the leadership positions she wanted, not just the ones she felt qualified for. She reached out to people who were where she aspired to be: mentors, leaders, and principals, and asked for advice. She began to speak up more in meetings and volunteer on high-visibility projects.

Weeks later, she walked into her interview with confidence; she didn't shrink herself. She stood tall and owned every answer with confidence. When they asked why she thought she was the right fit, she didn't hesitate with her answer.

And this time, there was no rejection e-mail. No, "*Thank you, but...*" e-mail, this time, there was a "Welcome to the team. Congratulations, Olivia."

She had stepped into her power, she had stopped waiting and started taking, and now there was no stopping her, because once she flipped the switch to beast mode, there was no going back.

Let's get this straight: Now that you're in beast mode, keeping promises to yourself isn't optional if you're serious. Every time you set a goal or commit to a routine, you're making a promise: not to your boss, family, or friends, but to yourself. Here's the deal: when you honor that commitment, it builds self-trust and confidence. When you break those promises, it chips away at your self-esteem, making it harder to believe in your ability to stay disciplined. Stop treating your goals like they're negotiable. Show yourself the same respect you would give someone you care about. When you follow through, you're telling yourself, 'I've got my own back,' and that's a powerful message.

Keeping your promises will require self-discipline. You can't hit the snooze. You have to ignore the knot in your stomach. You need to stop making excuses. It's here in that uncomfortable place where you begin to grow. Being self-disciplined is about owning every step of your journey, not avoiding it.

When you find yourself in moments that make you uncomfortable, look for an opportunity to grow and step out of your comfort zone. I believe that is why we see so many successful people under the age of 30. They don't have the same fear and trepidations as those of us who didn't grow up where everything was being recorded. Those of us over a certain age were always told not to overshare. The adults would say, "Don't you go in those streets telling people what happens in my house." For that reason, we have been stuck in a paradigm that may need to be shifted.

If you miss the mark, get up and keep going. One bad day doesn't erase all the progress you have made. Stay disciplined, stay focused. Your discipline will be your anchor, keeping you steady when the excitement of the class, the group, or the hype fades away. Discipline fights through not making excuses. When you stay the course, Success is inevitable.

To help you stay focused, establish habits that support the routines you need to stay on track. Set yourself up for success by making your goals knowledgeable. Have a plan. If you are working toward a fitness goal, schedule your workouts like appointments that you can't cancel. If you are building a new skill, set aside dedicated time every day to practice. Self-discipline will change how you see yourself. Every time you push past procrastination, fight through doubt, or show up when you don't feel like it, you're sending yourself a message that I can do this.

Daily habits are the secret weapon of self-discipline. Remember, beast mode isn't about perfection; it's about persistence. It's about showing up, even when it's hard, and trusting that every small step you take is building something bigger. It's about believing in yourself enough to keep your promises, push through discomfort, and stay committed to the process.

So, stop waiting for the perfect moment, the perfect family, or the perfect mood. It's not coming; what's here, right now, is your chance to step up and do the work to show yourself. Let's go!

I believe God has a plan for every single one of us, and no one can take what's divinely designed for you. Your purpose is not up for debate and sure isn't up for grabs. So let them do their thing while you stay locked in on yours. Trust that everything meant for you is already there.

Many times, when you're an overthinker, you begin to compare yourself in this moment because you think this can work for everyone but you. You may think I'm not good enough. Whatever negative thought that comes in, fight it. Don't try to compare yourself to anyone else because we are all different. Comparison is the thief of joy, and it will rob you blind. It will snatch away your happiness, confidence, and drive before you even realize what has happened. No one is more deserving or more worthy than you.

Remember, Beast Mode is about resilience, commitment, and showing up even when it's hard. It's about believing you're working toward something bigger and believing in yourself enough to keep your promises, push through discomfort, and stay committed to the process.

How do you build this resilience and commitment? You build it by creating small daily habits that create stability and momentum. Think of these as your personal power moves. When you create a routine, it can anchor your day in those moments when you don't feel motivated. You can start with simple routines: Set aside five or ten minutes every morning to focus on your intentions for the day or spend a few moments at night writing down something you're grateful for. These tiny, consistent actions might not seem like much, but over time, they add up and become automatic, grounding you when life's chaos throws you off course.

Having an accountability partner can be helpful by providing someone to check in with and discuss your goals or progress. Something that gets you hyped up! If you prefer to go alone. No problem, but make it fun. Tie it to something you love. For example, for your workout routine, get a fire playlist that will have you amped for the next hour or two. If you want to meditate. Grab a nice candle and your favorite blanket to make you feel comforted. Treat yourself to off days.

Whatever it is, these small steps chip away at any mental barriers that may stop you from moving forward.

Another way to boost confidence is to make decisions that align with your paradigm and values. When you do this and have that anchor for your choices, it makes it a whole lot easier to stand firm in the face of challenges.

If you're ready to level up, it's time to be bold. Being bold reminds you that you deserve to take up space, to express yourself, and pursue what sets your soul on fire. Every time you push past that hesitation, you boost your confidence. You're telling your brain: "I've got this." Confidence isn't about feeling doubt but refusing to let those feelings stop you. The more you show up for yourself, the more resilient and unshakable your confidence becomes.

Stepping outside of your comfort zone sends your soul a loud and clear message: *You Matter.* Every time you take that bold step of setting boundaries or speaking up for yourself, you are reinforcing your worth. Bold actions are declarations of self-respect.

Let's be honest: Beast Mode is uncomfortable. It pushes you out of the safety zone into the grit zone. But discomfort is where growth happens. That's where Olivia learned to stop shrinking in interviews and instead sit tall, own her worth, and speak her truth. That's where you'll learn to take the risk, say the thing, or start the project you've been avoiding.

And remember every rejection you've survived, every heartbreak you've endured, every setback you thought would break you, that's your evidence. That was your training ground. That's proof you can do hard things.

Stop waiting for the perfect moment. Stop comparing your lane to theirs. Stop telling yourself you'll start when you're ready. You're ready now. Beast mode isn't about perfection, it's about persistence. It's about showing up again and again, until your doubt has no choice but to bow down to your discipline.

Like Olivia, you have a choice today. You can stay stuck, hoping someone notices your worth. Or you can flip the switch, hit back, and prove to yourself that you are already Unstoppable!

It's your time. Step into the arena. Unleash Beast Mode. And don't look back!

Chapter 10

The Finishing Phase: Turning Pressure into Power

Pressure doesn't just make diamonds; it also bursts pipes. The difference? How you handle it.

When you're in the final stretch, everything feels heavier. The excitement of progress mixes with exhaustion, and fatigue whispers, "Maybe you can't finish this." Fear sneaks in too, not at the starting line, but here, when the finish line is in sight. That's when the pressure is at its peak. But here's the truth: pressure isn't here to crush you. It's here to crown you.

Cheryl knew this moment well. For years, she had been waiting for her chance to rise at work. She had the degree, the experience, the track record. But she also carried a quiet, heavy lie: "I'm not good enough." That belief had held her back, causing her to shrink in meetings, second-guess her ideas, and accept a background role when she was meant for the spotlight. But pressure has a way of forcing decisions. And Cheryl was done playing small.

Trust this: when you come out on the other side of this, you won't be the same person who started. You will be sharper, stronger, and the version of yourself that knows what it means to finish what you started.

The final stretch of any journey is a beast. You are this close to crossing the finish line, but suddenly, everything feels harder. You may feel exhausted, but fatigue isn't weakness; it's proof you've been in the fight. The heaviness you feel is the weight of every ounce of effort you've already poured in. Remember, you've been in Beast Mode. But here's the twist: Exhaustion and fear show up strongest right when you are about to break through.

Cheryl felt that weight too, sitting in her car outside the office, gripping the wheel, trying to summon the strength to walk in. She had been rejected before, overlooked before. But that day, she told herself, "I'm not letting exhaustion steal this moment."

And fear? Fear often sneaks up when success is within reach. It whispers, "What if I can't handle what comes next? What if I can't handle success? That fear is proof that you are on the right track. It wants to stop you and silence you. The truth is, success demands more from you: new responsibilities, higher expectations, and deeper resilience. That can be intimidating, but you are already becoming the person who can handle it. You've grown, and now you are the person who doesn't always have to be ready or have the perfect moment, but the person who can rise to the occasion and overcome challenges without shutting down or reverting to an old version of yourself.

Cheryl also experienced fear. She had applied for leadership roles before, half-heartedly, already bracing for rejection. But this time. She activated Beast Mode. She looked in the mirror and declared, "I am capable." I am worthy. I am enough." That shift? That was pressure turning into power.

Remember, pressure, fear, and doubt are emotions that can distract you from your game. Harness them into power to move forward and meet any challenge you face. The stakes may be high, but the outcome is worth it.

Remember, you are transforming. Every ounce of struggle, fatigue, or doubt is turning you into a stronger, sharper, more powerful version of yourself. This isn't just about reaching the finishing line; it's about showing yourself that you are Unstoppable.

Fear is a liar, and doubt is a thief. And if you let them run the show, they will rob you blind. Stealing your confidence, your drive, and your shot at success. But not today. Not anymore. Fear no longer dictates your next move.

So dig in, Push, and finish strong because when you're in Beast Mode, you don't quit, you conquer.

Visualize that finish line; you are locking in that win. When you visualize, feel every ounce of what you think it will feel like. The rush, the relief, every part of that experience. Who is with you? This isn't just a mental exercise; it's mental training; teaching your brain and body to expect success.

Remember, pressure isn't here to break you; it's here to build you. It's the weight that strengthens your mindset and resilience. But you must use it right. If you let pressure consume you, it will drain you, make you second-guess yourself, and leave you stuck in a cycle of stress and doubt. But if you learn to flip the script, that same pressure becomes your greatest fuel.

How do you transform pressure into fuel?

- **Break it down.** Big goals feel impossible in the final stretch. Slice them into mini goals. Every small win builds momentum.
- **Visualize the Finish.** Lock in your vision. Close your eyes. See yourself crossing the line. Feel the relief, the power, the pride. Train your brain to believe success is inevitable, not optional. Your brain doesn't know the difference.
- **Journal your fears.** Write down the doubts screaming in your head. Then ask: is this true? Where is the proof? You'll find most fear is nothing but noise.

Unstoppable: A 5 step Guide to Reclaiming Identity & Purpose

- **Stay accountable.** You're less likely to quit when someone's watching. Build a circle that checks in, pushes you, and celebrates your wins.
- **Celebrate small victories.** Don't wait for the "big goal." Every step forward is proof of your grit.

Cheryl did this. She stopped waiting for validation, started visualizing success, and held herself accountable by showing up differently at work. By the time she walked into her boss's office, she wasn't begging for approval. She was owning her next level. And she walked out with a promotion. Not because someone finally gave her a chance, but because she took it.

Let's get real: the closer you get to the finish, the more burnout tries to creep in. Burnout doesn't slam into you all at once; it sneaks in, disguised as exhaustion, frustration, or feeling "over it." The antidote? Balance. Rest isn't weakness; it's strategy. It's chess, not checkers. When you rest, you sharpen your blade, allowing you to cut through resistance with greater precision.

You have to learn to pace yourself; you're not a machine. Trying to power through without breaks will only slow you down in the long run. Schedule moments to reset; whether stepping away for a walk, blasting your favorite music, or just sitting in silence for a minute to breathe.

Beast Mode isn't about going 100 miles per hour 24/7. It's about knowing when to pace, when to sprint, and when to breathe. That rhythm keeps you in the game long enough to win it.

Celebrate your small wins. Remember, it's not just about reaching your goal but also about acknowledging how far you've come. Every step forward is a victory. If you finish a task you were dreading, celebrate it. Success is about every small step you take along the way. It's not just about reaching a goal, it's about who you become in the process. You aren't going to be the same person you were when you started this journey.

Unstoppable: A 5 step Guide to Reclaiming Identity & Purpose

You're tougher now. You've fought through doubt, faced fears, battled exhaustion, and you're still here. You kept going. That's what puts you in a league of your own.

Motivation may have started the race, but discipline will finish it. Discipline is that voice that pushes through. It helps you stay consistent, enabling you to show up even when you're in doubt, and even when no one applauds.

Find someone to help you stay accountable because you're less likely to slack when you know someone else is watching and rooting for you. Make it public and announce to everyone what you are trying to achieve. Track your habits with an app and create visual proof of your consistency. Seeing your progress will be just the fuel you need to get through another day.

The biggest driver of all will be your why. You have to remember the reason you are doing this so you can cross the finish line even when things get tough. The pressure may be intense, but this one little thing will help you avoid getting caught up in the opinions of others, the weight of deadlines, or endless possibilities.

Here's the final key: pressure only exists because what you're doing matters. You don't feel pressure when you're playing small. You feel pressure when the stakes are high, when the next level is calling, when your destiny is on the line. That pressure? It's proof that you're leveling up.

So when fear whispers, when fatigue weighs you down, when self-doubt creeps in, flip the script. Pressure isn't your enemy. It's proof that you're almost there.

You're in the final stretch. Can't you see the finish line from here? Don't you dare quit now.

Take a breath. Lock in. Push through. The pressure isn't here to crush you, it's here to crown you.

Like Cheryl, you've already proven you can rise. You've already shown grit. You've already fought to hard to stop now.

So finish strong. Celebrate victory. And then... Level Up because this isn't the end. It's just the launchpad.

BEAST MODE ACTIVATED!!!!! LET'S GOOOOOOOO!!!

Unstoppable: A 5 step Guide to Reclaiming Identity & Purpose

ABOUT THE AUTHOR

Jackie Hicks is an author, playwright, business strategist, and Enrolled Agent whose work spans creativity, empowerment, and financial leadership. As the founder of Powerful Echoes and a trusted consultant in taxation and business development, Jackie has helped countless entrepreneurs build confidence, clarity, and sustainable success. Her expertise blends strategic insight with a deep commitment to helping others transform their ideas into thriving realities.

Beyond her professional achievements, Jackie is a devoted wife, a storyteller, and a champion for women determined to reclaim the brilliance within themselves. Her journey into writing and empowerment work began with a simple but powerful truth: she was tired of seeing so many women second-guess their talents, underestimate their worth, or stay silent about their dreams. Jackie's mission became clear—create spaces, tools, and stories that remind women they are capable, powerful, and unstoppable.

Through her books, stages, consulting, and creative works, Jackie continues to amplify voices and expand possibilities. *Unstoppable* reflects her unwavering belief that when women recognize their own potential, they don't just change their lives—they change the world.

THERAPY RESOURCES

Going to therapy has helped me immensely in my life in recognizing patterns, habits, and beliefs that had me torn down and feeling defeated. I want to help as many people as I can. Here are the names of some mental health providers who may be able to assist you. I do not have references in every state, but the first one has providers nationwide. Many large employers offer this as a part of your benefits package, and your health insurance may also have this as a benefit. I hope you enjoyed the book if you did send an email and let me know to hickstable4u@gmail.com.

https://www.betterhelp.com/?frombhhealth=1

https://meagerbeginningsllc.com/ several states, call to find out if they are in yours

https://www.emotionalrx.com/ Florida

https://restcnc.com/ Florida

https://valeriecarmel.com/ Florida

References:

https://www.health.harvard.edu/staying-healthy/understanding-the-stress-response.
https://www.yourhormones.info/hormones/adrenaline/.
https://www.taniaflack.com/general/adrenal-exhaustion-are-you-surfing-on-adrenaline-what-are-the-long-term-effects/.
https://mhanational.org/what-adrenaline.

[1] https://www.egypttoday.com/Article/6/100785/15-Signs-It-Is-Time-to-Let-Go-of-Your

[2] https://lifesupportscounselling.com.au/resources/blogs/how-to-know-when-a-relationship-is-over-and-how-to-move-forwards-once-it-ends/

[3] https://www.lifebydesigntherapy.com/blog/11-warning-signs-that-your-personal-ambitions-are-putting-strain-on-your-relationship

[4] https://health.clevelandclinic.org/codependent-relationship-signs

[5] https://www.heartfeltcounselingmn.com/blog/2022/8/25/signs-your-relationship-is-in-a-communication-breakdown

[6] https://www.psychologytoday.com/us/blog/toxic-relationships/201904/signs-of-serious-relationship-problems

[7] https://www.psychologytoday.com/us/blog/think-act-be/202211/24-signs-relationship-is-likely-end

[8] https://www.today.com/life/relationships/relationship-red-flags-rcna52755

[1] https://www.riemannfamily.com/grief-support/who-am-i-now-grief-and-your-changing-identity

[2] https://www.myfarewelling.com/article/grief-and-identity-rediscovering-yourself-after-a-loss

[3] https://athenawellness.com/blog/2023/7/1/career-transition-grief-and-identity-loss

[4] https://www.griefrecoveryhouston.com/grief-recovery-center-method-deal-identity-changes-loss/

[5] https://pmc.ncbi.nlm.nih.gov/articles/PMC7370894/[6] https://whatsyourgrief.com/change-identity-loss-and-grief/

[7] https://www.compassionatefriends.org/blog/staying-afloat-when-grief-steals-your-identity/

https://lifesupportscounselling.com.au/resources/blogs/how-to-know-when-a-relationship-is-over-and-how-to-move-forwards-once-it-ends

Find More Resources

www.powerfulechoes.org

www. jacque.info

Use The Following Blank Pages for Notes. I hope you have lots of them and are motivated and encouraged throughout this book.

Unstoppable: A 5 step Guide to Reclaiming Identity & Purpose

Unstoppable: A 5 step Guide to Reclaiming Identity & Purpose

Unstoppable: A 5 step Guide to Reclaiming Identity & Purpose

Unstoppable: A 5 step Guide to Reclaiming Identity & Purpose

Unstoppable: A 5 step Guide to Reclaiming Identity & Purpose

Unstoppable: A 5 step Guide to Reclaiming Identity & Purpose

Unstoppable: A 5 step Guide to Reclaiming Identity & Purpose

Unstoppable: A 5 step Guide to Reclaiming Identity & Purpose

Made in the USA
Coppell, TX
13 January 2026